CULINARY HERBS

COMPLETE GARDENER'S LIBRARY™

CULINARY

HERBS

Maggie Oster

National Home Gardening Club
Minnetonka, Minnesota

Culinary Herbs

Printed in 2004.

Tom Carpenter
Creative Director

Julie Cisler
Book Design & Production

Michele Teigen
Senior Book Development Coordinator

Gina Germ
Photo Editor

Nancy Wirsig McClure, Hand to Mouse Arts
Julie Cisler
Illustration

Carole Saville
Contributing Writer

5 6 7 8 / 06 05 04
ISBN 1-58159-013-X
© 1998 National Home Gardening Club

National Home Gardening Club
12301 Whitewater Drive
Minnetonka, Minnesota 55343
www.gardeningclub.com

Photo Credits

Phil Aarrestad: cover; David Cavagnaro pp: i, 8, 18, 22, 23, 38 (2), 39, 40, 41, 42, 47, 60, 61, 62, 63, 66, 67, 68, 69 (2), 70, 75, 76, 79, 83 (2), 84, 85, 86, 87 (2), 91, 97, 101, 103, 104, 105, 107, 110, 112, 115, 116, 117, 118 both, 122 both, 124, 142, 147, 151; Jim Block pp: title, 6-7, 21, 61, 71, 77, 98, 100, 111, 114, 115, 121, 123, 133, 147, 150 both; Derek Fell pp: iii, 5, 18 (3), 19, 23 (2), 24-25, 27, 28, 29, 32, 35 (2), 56, 57, 65, 72, 73, 86, 87, 96, 107, 112, 113, 128, 135, 141, 149 (2); (Alan & Linda Detrick pp. 2-3; Walter Chandoha pp: 4 (2), 5, 9, 10 all, 11 all, 12 (2), 13, 15, 20, 22, 23, 27 (2), 28, 30, 33, 34 both, 35, 40, 41, 42, 44, 50-51, 55, 67, 74, 85, 90, 91, 93, 99, 100, 102, 103, 106, 113, 123, 124, 125, 131, 137, 139, 148; Saxon Holt pp: 4, 14, 44, 45, 58, 59, 141; Maggie Oster pp: 5, 19, 26, 27, 29 (2), 31 (2), 33, 38, 39 (2), 41, 45, 46, 47, 48, 49, 54, 55 (2), 56, 57, 59, 60, 63, 64, 66, 67, 69, 70, 71, 72, 75 (2), 77, 78, 80, 81, 82 (2), 85, 87, 89, 92, 93, 94, 95 all, 97, 101, 102, 105 (2), 108, 114, 116 (2), 117, 119, 121, 123, 125, 126, 127 (2), 128, 129, 130, 132, 133, 136, 139, 140, 142, 143, 145, 146, 149, 151; Bill Johnson pp: 15, 93, 141; Rosalind Creasy pp: 16-17, 21, 29, 30, 31, 36-37, 62, 63, 71, 74, 77, 78 (2), 79, 82, 83, 84, 85, 88, 89, 94, 98, 99, 109 both, 111, 114, 119, 120, 127, 129, 130, 131, 134, 135, 136, 138 both, 143, 144, 145, 148; Jim Cummins/FPG p: 19; Hugh Palmer pp. 19, 21, 93, 106, 145; Horticultural Photography, Mountain View, CA pp: 20, 90, 111, 117, 124, 125, 137, 143; David McGlynn/FPG p: 41; Patricia J. Bruno/Positive Images pp: 49, 133; Joseph G. Strauch, Jr. pp: 54, 65; Carole Saville p: 81; Michael Viard/Peter Arnold, Inc. pp: 126, 127

CONTENTS

ABOUT THE AUTHOR

Even though I've extensively grown, used and studied herbs for over 25 years, I continue to be astounded by how much better they make food taste. Even the simplest dish becomes something special when herbs are included. And herbs don't add fat or calories! Just flavor. Plus, many of them have health-giving benefits, as well.

When I first moved back to the Midwest from the East Coast two decades ago, only one place near where I lived sold herbs. Now every garden center and discount department store carries at least the basic culinary herbs, and many areas have at least one place that specializes in a wide range of herbs. There are wonderful mail-order companies that offer more herbs than you can imagine. This means that there is a wealth of opportunity to use and experiment with herbs from around the world.

Although I grow all kinds of plants, there is something particularly endearing about herbs. High on the list of reasons is that almost all of them are incredibly easy to grow, both in the garden and in containers. And it's possible to have most of my favorite herbs in a relatively small space. I also like the historical connection that herbs provide, plus the folklore that surrounds them. There is a quality to herbs, more than with any other plants, that is inherently soothing. Just walking among them in the garden calms me. And oh, those wonderful fragrances.

But because I am one of those people who lives to eat, it is what herbs bring to the table that is most important. Whether in a cold, refreshing drink in summer or a warming tea in winter, in a last-minute stir-fry or slow-simmering stew, added fresh to a salad or preserved in vinegar or a jar of jelly, herbs enrich my life with their flavor.

(Opposite) Utility doesn't preclude beauty, as evidenced by this planting of purple and sweet basil, curly parsley, garlic, lettuce, cabbage, dusty miller and amaranth.

Maggie Oster

CHAPTER 1

WHY GROW CULINARY HERBS?

Herbs are once more the fashion and everyone is planting them...they are very simple plants, requiring little attention, and if we do know how to use them, they reward us with many enjoyable hours.

—From *What to Do With Herbs*, 1939
Mary Cable Dennis

The most basic reason for growing a garden of culinary herbs, no matter how large or small, is simply that foods taste better when prepared with them. A handful of herbs from your own garden will taste much more flavorful than any cut herbs found in the produce section of most supermarkets these days.

As an example, consider parsley. It is available at the grocery every month of the year, so why grow this common herb in your garden? Try a little experiment. Grow your own parsley and conduct a taste test between garden-grown and store-bought. From that moment on, even parsley will become a staple in your yard.

With thoughtful planning, a garden that combines herbs, vegetables and flowers is a stunning addition to the landscape.

The warm, resinous accent of rosemary, the pleasingly hot, peppery bite of oregano and the cool, refreshing menthol in the dark green leaves of spearmint will perk up your foods with their myriad of flavors, making the herb gardener a creative cook, as well. In no time, you'll be finding ways to use herbs in all your cooking, adding depth of flavor to appetizers, soups, stews, casseroles, roasts, grilled foods, salads, vegetables, breads and muffins, your own specially formulated herb teas and even desserts.

You'll also gain a garden of fragrance. Consider the piney scent in the needle-like leaves of rosemary, the dusky scent of pebbly, gray-suede sage leaves or the clean, sweet aroma of lavender. In these days of praise for the benefits of aromatherapy to soothe the mind and body, nothing could be more rewarding than taking a walk on a hot summer day through your herb garden. Inhale the unique scents of the herbs intermingling with one another. Let yourself be engulfed by their perfume. Feel the sense of well-being in this peaceful, serene environment.

The process of designing and planning an herb garden gives you the opportunity to discover

Fresh herbs make even the simplest dish special. Be sure to experiment with different combinations of herbs.

Growing herbs gives you the opportunity to try your hand at creative gardening techniques, such as making a topiary from rosemary.

Store-bought can't begin to compare to home-grown, vine-ripened tomatoes just waiting for some fresh basil.

but it has a special kind of beauty in its textures and colors. You'll become aware of the many shades of green, the different textures and patterns of foliage and the variety of plant sizes and shapes. There are, however, many herbs with colorful foliage or flowers. With careful planning, even the the most utilitarian herb garden can have flair and a wide-ranging palette.

In this book you will find a selection of culinary herbs and edible flowers that will undoubtedly deliver flavor as well as create beauty in the gar-

den. Many of the culinary herbs are hardy, long-lived perennials. Plus they are relatively carefree. So enter the world of culinary herbs—filled with flavor, fragrance and beauty.

With ready access to herbs, you'll find lots of ways to use them. Besides dill in pickles, think about making herbal jellies and other preserved treats for yourself or to give as gifts.

another aspect of your creative side. Themes for herb garden designs are boundless, allowing the imagination much play. Some of these possibilities are:

• A period garden, such as the geometrically patterned, formal style of a Medieval garden.
• A garden where herbs are mixed with flowering annuals and roses.
• A colorfully jumbled cottage garden.
• A vegetable garden with carefully chosen herbs as companion plants.
• A garden with a monochromatic color scheme.
• A garden of lemon-scented herbs with a lemon tree as a centerpiece.

A final reason for developing an herb garden is that it is beautiful. Maybe not a flashy beauty, as with a flower border,

Chive flowers not only are beautiful but also edible, as are many other herb flowers. Look for creative ways to use herb flowers in the landscape and in the kitchen.

# ◀ CHAPTER 2 ▶
A PRACTICAL GUIDE
TO GROWING HERBS

Tending a garden of culinary herbs establishes a link with the distant past. Many of the plants we grow in our present-day gardens for their flavor and scent were also grown and enjoyed by gardeners in ancient times for the same reasons. All of those gardeners before you trod the same path—inhaling the sweet scent of lavender, savoring the bite of watercress and the tartness of sorrel, being seduced by the clove-like taste of basil, and drifting off to sleep after a warming cup of dill tea. These gardeners surely shared the same issues of preparing the soil, pulling weeds and all the other tasks that ensure bounty from the herb garden. This link to the past is a comforting one, as you realize that in the time spent among your herbs you are taking part in the continuity of the soul-enriching art of herb gardening.

THE BEST ENVIRONMENT

Choose a site for the herb garden that gets at least five or six hours of direct, unobstructed sun each day, as this is best for the majority of herbs. If you have a choice, a site with morning sun is preferable to one with afternoon sun. There are a few herbs that require or tolerate partial shade, such as the mint family, which will thrive in the dappled light created by tall trees with open branching.

The soil requirement for growing healthy herbs is generally an average to moderately fertile soil that contains organic matter. Being well-supplied with organic matter helps the soil provide nutrients, retain moisture and allow good aeration.

There are three basic types of soil. Loam is the most desirable. It is a well-balanced mix of sand, silt and clay particles. Even when moist, a handful will readily crumble between your fingers. Clay soil is rich in nutrients but it has poor drainage and aeration; pick up some when it's wet and it will form a firm ball in your hand. Sandy soil is porous but unable to hold nutrients and water for long.

Interestingly enough, adding organic matter improves all three soils. Among the organic amendments to improve the soil are homemade or purchased compost, well-composted animal manures, peat moss, pulverized bark and mushroom compost.

Make an evaluation to determine the nutrient levels in the area where the garden is to be planted. That way you'll know exactly how much nitrogen, phosphorus and potassium you have to add, if any. Local nurseries can usually provide soil-testing kits or the names of nearby soil-testing laboratories. Your local agricultural county extension office also offers assistance with analyzing your soil.

Check the pH level of your soil, too, as it influences how well plants absorb nutrients. The ideal pH level varies from plant to plant, but most herbs do best with a pH of 6.5 to 7.0. Adding agricultural limestone to the soil raises the pH, while ground sulfur lowers it.

Adding organic matter (such as compost or well-aged manure) is the best thing you can do for your garden, no matter what your soil type.

Making your own compost saves money and recycles yard waste, such as grass clippings in spring and summer or leaves in the autumn.

Most culinary herbs do not need a soil as rich as perennials or roses do. The soil should not be so poor in nutrients that the herbs don't grow well; if the soil is too rich, the growth will be luxurious but with only small amounts of the flavorful essential oils. Only those herbs that are heavily harvested, such as basil, benefit from a rich soil.

In choosing fertilizers to add to the soil, remember that the amount and ratio of the major nutrients—nitrogen, phosphorus and potassium—is printed on the packages. Follow the directions printed on the packages.

Inorganic fertilizers generally provide nutrients to the plant roots immediately and are available in liquid or dry form, timed-release pellets, stakes, sticks or tablets. Organic fertilizers are better for herbs because they naturally release the nutrients slowly over the growing season. Organic fertilizers are commercially available that contain balanced amounts of nitrogen, phosphorus and potassium, as are products that supply each of these nutrients individually.

ADVANCE SOIL PREPARATION—THE KEY TO SUCCESS

Nothing is more important to the successful growth of plants than proper advance soil preparation. Skip this all-important first step and you're asking for trouble. Abide by it and you've taken a huge step in ensuring a thriving, easy-to-care-for garden.

No matter what type of soil you have, from the lightest sand to the heaviest clay, a liberal addition of organic matter works miracles. Organic matter can be anything from compost to well-rotted leaf mold, fine fir bark or peat moss. Almost every area of the country lays claim to indigenous, inexpensive organic material that is readily available to gardeners.

A good rule-of-thumb is that the amount of organic matter

you add should be equal to the depth to which you intend to turn the soil. If you're preparing the soil for raised beds, the minimum depth you should till is 6 inches; 8 to 12 or more inches is that much better. This may contradict some traditional advice, but the rule has proved to be very successful.

If you intend to till the soil to a depth of 8 inches, then you should add 8 inches of organic material on top of the soil before you till to incorporate it to the full depth. This takes some doing, but it helps your plants develop an extensive, healthy root system. This results in a hardy, vigorous and productive garden that is able to withstand

periods of drought and resist diseases and pests.

Depending on what you're planting and the characteristics of your soil, you may want to add fertilizer and lime as you incorporate the organic matter. Explain your situation to your local nursery staff or extension agent to find out more about fertilizer recommendations.

After tilling the organic matter into the soil, rake the area smooth and plant your plants. Keep the area well-watered for the first few weeks after planting. You'll be amazed at the growth of the plants in such superior soil, even in the first year.

GETTING STARTED

Egg cartons are an inexpensive option for starting seeds. Just be sure to punch some drainage holes in the bottom before filling with seed-starting mix.

A seed-starting kit with a plastic cover provides the high humidity environment that helps ensure successful seed germination.

Buying herbs at the nursery or from specialty mail order nurseries is the easiest, quickest and most "instantly gratifying" manner in which to start your herb garden.

Many gardeners, however, simply enjoy the magic of the birth process of growing herbs from seed. Another reason to start herbs from seeds is if you need a large amount of certain herbs, perhaps as a ground cover or to sell to restaurants or at the local farmer's market. This is when propagating herbs from seed is the most economical. Starting seeds indoors, rather than out, is usually more reliable, too.

Starting Seeds Indoors

Don't take chances and get too early a jump on the gardening season by sowing seeds indoors in early winter. Sowing seeds indoors about six, and no more than eight, weeks before the last expected frost date is a good rule of thumb to follow in order to produce healthy transplants. Proper light, nutrients and watering are the three necessities for successfully starting and growing seeds indoors.

In an ideal world, a greenhouse is the best place to grow seedlings. A diligent gardener can, however, grow seedlings in a window facing south- or southeast if there are no buildings or other obstructions outside blocking the light. Fluorescent light fixtures, fitted either with grow lights or equal numbers of cool-white and warm-white tubes, are another alternative. Light units that hold four fluorescent tubes are best.

When ready to sow seeds, use clean pots or plastic or fiber flats filled with a lightweight, commercial seed-starting mixes. Moisten the mix well with warm

If using a makeshift cover, such as a plastic bag, provide some type of support so that it doesn't touch the leaves.

water before filling the container. Plant seeds at the depth specified in the directions on the seed packet, then label each row of seeds with the name of the herb and planting date. Mist the soil surface with a very fine spray. Cover with a plastic dome lid, a piece of clear plastic or a sheet of glass; remove this covering when the seedlings emerge.

When the first set of true leaves appear, transplant the seedlings to small clean pots filled with moistened potting soil. When ready to go outdoors, the plants must be hardened off, a rather harsh sounding term that simply means to gradually acclimatize them in increments to their new outdoor environment. Here's how:

Initially, place the pots of herbs in a spot that is sheltered from sun and wind. Bring them indoors to spend the night for the first few days, then allow them to spend the night outdoors. In the same careful manner, gradually expose them to full sun, or if they are shade-loving herbs, to that environment.

Set transplants where you want them in the garden before planting, allowing enough space between them for plenty of growing room.

Gather ripe seed from herbs and store in an airtight container in a cool, dark place for planting next spring.

Starting Seeds Outdoors

Directly sowing seeds into the ground outdoors is recommended for annuals that grow quickly or herbs that do not transplant well. Cilantro, chervil, dill and fennel are among the herbs that readily grow from seed sown outdoors.

To start seeds outdoors, wait until all danger of frost is past. Sow the seeds in well-prepared soil at the depth specified on the seed packet. Broadcast tiny seeds on top of the soil, then cover with fine, sifted soil or vermiculite. Tamp the soil gently and soak with a soft, gentle spray of water.

As the first sets of true leaves develop, thin the seedlings so that each one has room to grow without being crowded by the other seedlings. Seasoned gardeners are ruthless about removing seedlings in order to space plants properly. If you are reluctant to remove seedlings, put them to good use in your dinner salad. To prevent disturbing the roots of the remaining plants, clip off the thinnings at ground level with a scissors.

In thinking about starting seeds, don't overlook the "second gardening season" (mid to late summer) for autumn harvest. Plant seeds of basil, calendula, chamomile, chervil, chives, dill, parsley or sorrel between June and August, depending on the climate, for a lush fall harvest.

Buying herb transplants at a nursery or garden center gives you the opportunity to have an "instant" herb garden.

Annual, Perennial, Biennial?

Culinary herbs are annual, perennial or biennial plants.

An annual plant completes its life cycle in one season: it germinates, flowers, sets seed and dies. Hardy annual herbs such as dill are those that will withstand some frost and freezing temperatures. Many of these hardy annuals self-sow in the garden after they bloom and set seed. Gardeners may sow hardy annuals in the fall so that the young plants can put down good root growth in the still-warm earth, then emerge a sturdy plant early next spring. Tender annual plants such as basil are those that do not survive frost or freezing temperatures. They are sown in the garden when all danger of frost is past. They may also be sown indoors six weeks before the last frost date, then transplanted to the garden after the frost date.

Perennials such as sage are plants that continue to grow and bloom year after year, perhaps dying back in the winter but returning each spring from the same root system. Tender perennials are those that do not survive frost or freezing weather. These need to be brought indoors during the winter. Hardy perennials survive varying amounts of cold weather, as indicated by their Hardiness Zone number.

Biennial plants germinate in the spring, produce leafy growth during the summer and bloom the following spring or summer.

PROPAGATING HERBS

Layering, whether in the garden or from container to container, is an effective way to propagate some woody, flexible-stemmed herbs.

Stem cuttings are a simple method for producing more plants for your garden or to share with friends. This is also the most common method for propagating herbs that do not come true from seed.

With a pair of very sharp scissors or pruning shears, take 4- to 6-inch cuttings from the young, leafy tips of herb stems or branches. Cut just below where a leaf joins the stem, a point that is called the leaf node. Remove the leaves from the lower half of the cutting. Place each stem in a glass of water on a windowsill that receives bright but not direct sunlight. Change the water daily, and when the roots are ¼-inch long, plant the cuttings in a pot of moistened potting mix. Place the pots of rooted cuttings in a tray and cover them with clear plastic. Place the tray in an area with bright light but not direct sun. Or place them under fluorescent or high-intensity grow lights. Open the plastic cover regularly to provide air circulation. Mist the plants with a fine spray daily. Keep the soil evenly moist. When new top growth appears, remove the pots from the container and set them in a shady spot outdoors for several days to harden off.

You can also start the rooting process in pots of moistened perlite, vermiculite or coarse sand. Take cuttings as described above, then dip the stems in a rooting hormone powder. Make an indentation in the rooting mixture with a pencil and carefully insert the stem. Firm the mixture around the stem. Cover the pots with clear plastic and care for the cuttings as explained previously. After several weeks, gently tug at the stems. If you feel a slight resistance, you know that the cuttings are rooted and ready to be transplanted to individual pots.

Division is the method of propagation often used with perennial herbs. This is best done in early spring or at the end of the growing season. Dig up the entire plant and divide the root mass into several clumps. Sometimes the roots pull apart with your fingers, but with some plants, you'll have to pry the roots apart with a spade

When layering a plant, it's important to keep the stem in contact with the soil, either with a small stone or with a wire "hairpin."

Stem Cuttings

With sharp scissors or pruning shears, cut a 4- to 6-inch piece of stem.

Gently remove the leaves from the lower half of the cutting.

To speed rooting, dip the bare stem in rooting hormone powder.

Division

To divide a plant, dig it up, getting a large section of the root ball.

Pull plant sections apart, making sure there is top growth on each one.

If the roots can't be pulled apart, cut them apart with a sharp knife.

or cut them with a knife. Plant the divisions immediately. If this is not possible, wrap them in wet newspaper and transplant as soon as possible.

Layering is a quick and relatively effortless method for propagating herbs. It is especially

good for rosemary, sage or thyme, as their stems easily root while still attached to the parent plant. To layer, choose a vigorous branch that is growing close to the ground. Scrape off a half-inch portion on the side of the stem closest to the ground, or cut halfway through the stem at an angle. Carefully bend the branch to the ground and bury the scraped or cut portion in the soil, holding it in place with an old-fashioned clothespin or a bent piece of wire. Gently bend the end of the growing tip up vertically and support it with a small stake. When the stem has roots, sever it from the parent plant. Then carefully dig it up and transplant.

Once the newly layered plant develops roots, it is severed from the "parent" and grown in the pot or transplanted into the garden.

Layering

Nick a small section of the stem, secure it in the soil and support the tip.

When rooted and growing, cut the stem between the two plants.

Immediately transplant the layered plant to another spot in the garden.

Make an indentation in the moistened rooting mix and insert the cutting.

Cover the cuttings with clear plastic that is supported above the cuttings.

Herb Garden Care

Water herbs when the top inch of soil is dry. If you want to, you can add a liquid fertilizer or compost tea at the same time.

Shredded bark is one of the most commonly available mulches, but it can shed water. Counteract this problem by mixing in compost or shredded leaves.

An organic mulch (such as compost, finely chipped bark or shredded leaves) slows down the evaporation of soil moisture, inhibits weed growth and adds nutrients to the soil when it decomposes. Plus it keeps soil from splashing up on the leaves and makes the garden more attractive.

The mulch you choose often depends on cost and availability. Shred leaves in the autumn with a lawn mower or leaf shredder and store until spring. Fine-textured compost is another good choice. Don't use materials that mat or shed water, such as grass clippings or a thick layer of shredded bark. One way to use bark, since it is so readily available, is to mix it with finer material like compost or shredded leaves. If weeds are severe, lay down sheets of newspaper on the ground first, then cover with mulch.

Spread the mulch around the plants in spring after the soil has warmed up and is moist from rain. Make the mulch layer about 2 to 3 inches deep. Leave several inches unmulched around the base of the plant to prevent rot.

If you live in an area with extended periods of cool, damp weather, it's better to use a fine-gravel mulch for the gray-leaved herbs and the woody ones from

Water and Mulch

Although good drainage is essential for most culinary herbs (some are even drought tolerant), it is still important to supply adequate moisture. When supplemental watering is necessary, be sure to water slowly and deeply. The roots of plants seek water as deeply as it is available to them. Therefore, deep watering produces well-anchored plants that are better able to fend for themselves. A good rule of thumb is to allow the top inch of soil to become dry. If that occurs and no rain is expected, then water thoroughly.

An organic mulch not only makes the garden more attractive, but keeps weeding to a minimum, conserves moisture and gradually adds nutrients.

around the Mediterranean, such as thyme or rosemary.

Controlling Pests

Fortunately for herb gardeners, pests are seldom an overwhelming problem, as the very scents that attract humans to fragrant herbs are offensive to many insects. However, some of the pests that occasionally bother herbs are ants, aphids, scale, spider mites and slugs. You can control all these critters (except the slugs) with sprays of horticultural soap.

Everyone has their own particular method for battling slugs without using harmful chemicals. One method is to lay a short board in the garden at night, then destroy the accumulated slugs underneath early the next morning. Another method is to put crushed eggshells or horticultural grade diatomaceous earth around the base of the herbs, as slugs won't crawl over these.

Mildew and rust are the two diseases that might occur. These are apt to be prevalent if plants are spaced too closely or there is another reason for poor air circulation. Cut back or remove diseased plants.

Winter Care

In colder regions, many of the perennial herbs benefit from some form of winter protection. This is especially beneficial in areas that alternate between cold and warm periods during the winter, as these conditions cause plants to be heaved out of the ground from repeated freezing and thawing. Snowcover is the cheapest care method, but there are other possibilities, particularly in regions where snow is not a regular occurrence. More reliable is to put a loose layer of pine boughs over the plants after the ground freezes hard. You can also use leaves that don't pack down, such as oak, to cover

plants during the winter. Of course, it is important before planting to make sure your herb garden will not be subjected to strong winter winds.

Because of the essential oils in the leaves, herbs are seldom bothered by pests. If they do invade, try to wash them off with water or use a food-safe control such as horticultural soap spray. (Shown: aphids.)

‹ CHAPTER 3 ›

THE ART OF USING HERBS IN THE GARDEN

The design of an herb garden is limited only by the gardener's imagination. Consider how a culinary herb garden fits into your lifestyle, beginning with how much time and money you can or wish to devote to the garden.

Perhaps you are a romantic and envision a cottage garden with billowing herbs spilling over the edges of a path. But billowing herbs may spell "untidy" to another gardener, who envisions a more controlled appearance to the garden. Others may like the look or ease of planting the kitchen herbs along with the vegetables, so all the culinary plants are in one area. Formal gardens designed in geometric patterns appeal to some, while theme gardens featuring a particular subject entice others.

From another perspective, it is not necessary to create a separate herb garden to be able to enjoy culinary herbs. Instead "a garden *with* herbs" can be designed, for these adptable plants easily fit into most parts of the yard. Herbs blend in handsomely in foundation plantings, beds or borders of annual and perennial flowers or in special situations, such as an underutilized side yard.

A Formal Herb Garden

The beauty of a formal herb garden, with geometric beds surrounding a central element such as a topiary, fountain, small tree, sundial or sculpture, lies not only in its elegant simplicity but in its utilitarian aspects. The adage "form follows function" most certainly applies to this style of garden.

By planting the beds no more than 3 feet wide, it is easy to reach the herbs. Plus, the gardener never has to set foot onto the soil while seeding, weeding, cultivating and harvesting the herbs, so there is no danger of compacting the soil once it is prepared.

Design the pathways wide enough to get a wheelbarrow through. Paths are usually of a material that is pleasant to walk on, such as smooth river stone, bark chips, grass or brick.

Formal gardens often feature raised beds, perhaps surrounded by brick or Belgian block laid on edge, stone or untreated wood. Raised beds ensure that the herbs have good drainage.

Mirroring halves are the key to formal garden design. A focal point and surrounding hedge or fence are other important elements.

The individual beds may contain whatever the gardener desires. Each bed could hold a mixture of culinary herbs, a single species or several species of one genus. Another way is to give each bed its own theme. For instance, one bed might be edible flowers, another could have salad ingredients, while still another could be planted with herbs that have flowers of the same color.

For a softer appearance, the beds in a formal garden can have curving edges, but they should be well-defined, such as with this brick edging.

The formal garden may be enclosed by a hedge, perhaps of English or Korean boxwood, or surrounded by a wooden fence or a brick or stone wall. Other possibilities for enclosing the garden include a woven wattle fence or espaliered fruit trees.

Formal gardens need not be complicated. These beds are narrow enough that you can reach the plants in the center. Plus the paths easily accommodate equipment and the low wall defines the space.

A tall sheared hedge creates a "secret garden" atmosphere, and the potted dwarf peach draws the eye as the focal point of this garden.

Here, a gazebo creates a dramatic focal point. This colonial garden illustrates that formal design isn't limited to grand homes.

A fountain brings another dimension of sound and movement to the garden, drawing both the eyes and ears to the focal point.

Focal Points

There is an adage among gardeners that "strong lines equal good design." A key component of a strong garden design is a singular focal point to which the eye is naturally drawn. A strategically placed element in the garden creates the illusion of depth and space. The intent is to create visual interest via perspective, so that the illusion is of a distant oasis. It doesn't matter if the garden area isn't large. The trick is to give the *illusion* that it is large by creating a sense of depth.

In a formal garden, the focal point is traditionally placed in the center of the garden, but it could also be placed in the center of one side. For a more informal garden style, the focal point takes its place away from the center. It might be in one corner or sited a third of the way along a border.

The focal point can be anything that the gardener desires, from a serious sculpture to the frivolity of found art. It might be as grand as a gabled gazebo or spectacular waterfall. Or, it can be as simple as a wooden bench or old-fashioned gazing globe on a pedestal.

A classic birdbath situated as a focal point is both utilitarian and pleasurable, providing endless entertainment from watching the birds who venture there. Remember to keep it filled with fresh water. Surround it with herbs such as bee balm that provide nectar for butterflies and hummingbirds.

A water garden as a focal point represents a cool and restful oasis, beckoning the viewer to come and sit a spell at water's edge. Just a few container plants, such as the airy gracefulness of lemon grass or a carefully trained herbal topiary, add additional interest. To give more depth to a water garden focal point, include stepping

An antique wellhead centers this garden, much as it might have in a traditional formal Medieval herb garden.

stones leading the eye and foot up to it.

A dome-shaped, woven bee skep makes a traditional focal point, especially when placed in a bed of bee-attracting herbs or heirloom flowers. It is equally at home in an old-fashioned cottage garden or in the vegetable garden, perhaps nestled in among low-growing culinary herbs like thyme or marjoram.

A lovely old cast-iron urn acts as a focal point here. Placing a bench in the corner of the garden is a centuries-old tradition.

INTEGRATING HERBS WITH FLOWERS

Lavender, artemisia, sage, thyme, feverfew, tansy and yarrow combine with daylilies, cabbage, dahlias, roses and marigolds in this cottage garden.

The purple flowers of catmint make a stunning edging to a border with alternate plantings of lavender-flowered German iris and purple sage.

Culinary herbs readily fit in with plantings of perennials, annuals, roses or other plants. For instance, a large clump of oregano is effective as an anchor in a bed of colorful deep-purple lobelia and acid-yellow violas. The pale lavender cotton-ball flowers of chives perfectly complement the soft mauve of an 'Angel Face' rose, with pink-flowering geraniums planted nearby.

The texture of the foliage of many herbs is the perfect foil to flowering ornamentals. Try the frilly leaves of curly parsley combined with the gigantic, wrinkled, claret-red leaves of red mustard and the fresh-faced flowers of purple-and-white-petaled 'Cuty' viola.

Don't forget that many herbs have showy flowers, too. The decorative qualities of feathery-foliaged dill, fennel, caraway, anise or cilantro make stunning combinations with ornamentals. For instance, the broad yellow umbels of 'Fernleaf' dill make a terrific combination when planted next to golden-hued gloriosa daisies. White-flowering herbs planted between colorful flowers make them stand out in the border. Planting white-flowered winter savory between butter-yellow 'Lemon Gem' marigolds makes the blossoms all the more "buttery."

Even in a small garden, you can create the illusion of space by planting large-foliaged herbs in front of the border, with the smaller-leaved ones in the back; this gives a sense of depth. Another way to emphasize depth is by placing brilliantly colored flowers and herbs toward the front and blue flowers and blue-green foliage toward the back.

The honey-scented white flowers of garlic chives are the perfect foil for brightly colored annuals like marigolds, impatiens and scarlet sage.

The abundantly blooming bergamot, or bee balm, is often first thought of as an ornamental perennial rather than an herb, but both its flowers and leaves have a citrus-mint flavor.

COLORFUL FOLIAGE

The leaves of herbs offer an amazing range of colors and hues of green, silver, gray, purple or bronze. In addition, there are many variegated forms. Blue-green leaves provide restful color. Silvers and grays combined with pastel-flowering herbs and ornamentals provide romance in the garden. Utilizing the various shades of green foliage in combination with hot-colored flowers or brightly variegated herbs provides a garden with excitement.

Purple-, red- or bronze-leaved herbs (such as the purple forms of sage and perilla, 'Opal' or 'Red Rubin' basil or bronze fennel) particularly highlight silver-colored foliage like that of lavender, curry plant, southernwood, wormwood or lamb's-ears. These dark-hued herbs also complement blue-green foliage, giving the illusion of a cooler environment. 'African Blue' basil, with its burgundy-colored striations, is effective with both other burgundy-colored plants and plants with burgundy flowers.

Herbs with variegated foliage create complex punctuation in the garden. Some of the brightly variegated plants include golden bay, pineapple mint, ginger mint, variegated lemon balm, 'Alaska' nasturtiums, 'Prince Rupert' scented geranium, variegated myrtle, golden oregano, 'Golden Rain' rosemary, golden and tricolor sages and several different forms of variegated thyme.

Cream-, white- or yellow-variegated foliage effectively provides a "headlight" effect in the garden, especially when combined with plants with dark green leaves. For instance, the shimmering leaves of variegated silver thyme make a lovely foil for the deep-throated flowers of

Purple and yellow-variegated sages plus silver-leaved santolina accent the geometric spaces created with trimmed boxwood in this parterre garden.

'Blue Bedder' penstemon and exuberant white alyssum.

Or, make an entire planting a hotbed of color by combining 'Crystal Bowl Yellow' pansies, yellow calendula, golden oregano and golden thyme. Adding English lavender, with its soft mauve flowers, provides contrast. The royal-robe purple of 'Universal' pansies creates a stunning accent.

The deeply colored leaves of purple basil complement the bright green leaves of sweet basil and the lavender flowers of anise hyssop.

Golden-leaved thyme contrasts with a dark-leaved thyme surrounding the steps in this garden path. Both herbs release a lovely scent.

INTEGRATING HERBS INTO THE LANDSCAPE

A small but beautifully designed herb garden, complete with pineapple finial and bee skep, welcomes visitors. The stone edging and wall repeats the use of stone in the house and fence.

society garlic, with the pale lavender flowers complementing the deep purple blossoms of the potato vine. The other one is underplanted with Santa Barbara daisy. A complementary touch of purple is reflected in the sumptous sage planted with the upright French thyme in a sea-green strawberry jar beneath one of the solanums.

To further enrich the color scheme, a pink-flowering 'Bonica' rose scrambles along one side of the fence. Richly textured herbs, such as curly parsley and nutmeg-scented geranium, lend immediate interest and fragrance to the entry garden. A rounded clump of dark green thyme and the grassy chives soften one edge of the path, while the striking variegation of golden thyme

Integrating Herbs Along a Driveway

Often there is underutilized garden space along the side of the driveway. A border of herbs alone or combined with ornamental flowers and shrubs serves a couple purposes: It makes a welcoming decorative border to the driveway and flavors your food as well.

Integrating Herbs into the Entry Garden

The garden shown at the beginning of this chapter shows a planting packed with herbs, ornamental flowers and shrubs. This design provides a welcome-mat environment, beckoning the visitor to come in. In this garden, there are two anchoring ornamental

potato vine standards on either side of the path. One is underplanted with large clumps of

Knot gardens became popular in Elizabethan times. A bay topiary is the perfect centerpiece to this knot of rosemary, hyssop, red barberry and curly parsley.

Many gardeners like to plant their herbs near the vegetables so that both can be gathered at once when getting ready to prepare a meal.

Stepping stones lead one among the herbs in a cottage-style garden overflowing with a wide array of herbs and other plants.

and golden sage planted in pots soften the opposite edge of the entry. Orange-flowered nasturtium spill cheerfully from a terra cotta pot, giving colorful punctuation to this area. With this level of interest at the entry garden, who could resist exploring the path beyond?

Theme Gardens

Theme gardens are an entertaining way to incorporate herbs into your landscape. What about an Elizabethan knot garden planted with garlands of three or four herbs of complementary colors and textures, with each clipped into a tidy intertwining hedge? For those who can't get enough herb tea, how about a tea garden using only herbs that make soothing herbal infusions?

Among the other possibilities are a native American herb garden, a Colonial herb garden surrounded by a picket fence, a butterfly garden planted with herbs attracting these fluttery creatures, a garden devoted solely to herbs of a certain flower color or a garden all of silver and gray foliage.

My start on the road to gardening with herbs was with several cuttings from a "friendship garden". Each of the herbs passed on to me was originally from other friends. Sharing plants is a most pleasurable and enduring way to give and receive, and carry on the herb garden tradition.

Even the smallest area can become an herb garden, such this spot along a fence. Here you will find scented geraniums, mints, lavender, thyme, heliotrope, lemon grass, basil and a miniature rose.

A Medieval-themed garden includes herbs, vegetables and fruit trees in beds set among well-defined paths. The woven wattle fence adds another authentic touch.

⊲ CHAPTER 4 ⊳
THE ART OF GROWING HERBS IN CONTAINERS

Whatever the allotted garden space, an area of artfully potted herbs can bring pleasure and satisfaction to the most ardent herb gardener. The reasons for growing herbs in containers are many.

Perhaps you have no yard at all or only a patio or balcony. Or, maybe the available growing area contains unsuitable soil that is too much trouble or expense to amend. Then, sometimes, the reason is simply that the passion for herbs is so great that there is no room left in the garden for "just one more herb."

For gardeners with physical disabilities, potted plants placed at a height to suit the gardener minimize bending. Placed on stands with wheels, containers become portable—allowing them to follow the sun's path. Weed-free gardening is a reality as well. And containers of herbs are an excellent way to introduce childen to gardening.

Many gardeners use containers to trial newly discovered herbs to observe the growing habits before placing them elsewhere in the garden. Tender herbs are often summered outdoors in containers, then brought in for the winter. And some people grow herbs in containers just because they want to!

CONTAINER POSSIBILITIES

Unglazed terra cotta pots, whether plain or decorated, are widely available and offer the benefit of good aeration for roots. But bring these pots indoors in winter.

In choosing containers for growing herbs, select ones that please you aesthetically and financially, fit in best with the rest of your landscape and adequately accommodate the plants.

Whether you grow herbs from seed or buy young transplants, use the houseplant principle of not putting a small plant in a large pot. As the plants grow larger, transplant them into increasingly bigger pots. Ideally, the final container is large enough for the herb's roots to grow, permit good drainage and provide for air and water circulation.

Unglazed terra cotta, concrete or untreated wood containers are porous, allowing for plenty of air in the soil and helping the water to evaporate efficiently. Before adding potting mix, soak

HYPERTUFA CONTAINERS

Lightweight hypertufa containers, made from a mixture of Portland cement, peat moss and vermiculite, mimic old, weathered stone. These make rustic containers for herbs. Hypertufa troughs are available at nurseries and garden centers but are expensive, so if you're the do-it-yourself type, you can make your own.

The materials needed are a mold, a piece of plastic, sphagnum peat moss (either shredded or long-fibered), horticultural perlite or vermiculite, Portland cement, fibermesh (shredded fiberglass for strengthening concrete), a mixing container and pencils or 3/8-inch dowel rods. Concrete coloring is optional. Most of these items are available at hardware or building-supply stores.

First, choose a mold for your

container. This might be a plastic dishpan, cardboard box or wet sand. Cover the mold completely with a large piece of plastic, such as a garbage bag. Eliminate as many wrinkles in the plasic as possible. Your container can be formed on the inside or the outside of the mold, depending on the mold and the desired final size.

In the mixing container, combine one part peat moss, one part perlite or vermiculite, two parts cement and one handful of fibermesh (more or less depending on the final size). Add enough water to make the mixture into a stiff consistency. It should hold its shape without water pooling on the surface.

Start patting the moist mixture onto the mold. Make the bottom about 2 inches thick, and be sure

it is perfectly level. Make the sides at least 1 inch thick, although 1 1/2 to 2 inches is sturdier. Insert pencils or dowel rods in the bottom to create drain-age holes, leaving them in place.

Set the container in a dry place, such as a garage or basement. Let it dry for three days, misting daily to keep the surface barely moist. Let it sit another two days, then remove the container from the mold. Remove the pencils or dowel rods and make sure the holes are still open. Some people like to carve designs in the sides with a chisel or rough them up with a wire brush at this stage.

The final drying takes another two to four weeks, depending on the weather. The container is completely dry when it sounds hollow when tapped.

Wooden containers, such as these half barrels, can be left outdoors during winter. Stain them or leave them to weather naturally.

these porous containers in water so that they do not wick moisture from the soil. Terra cotta pots must be stored indoors in a dry place during the winter to prevent them from freezing and breaking. Do not use treated wood with any edible plant, including herbs.

Plastic or glazed ceramic containers are nonporous and do not permit free passage of air and water. With these containers, good drainage is essential and care must be taken not to overwater.

Herbs look delightful in "collectible" containers, too, such as whimsical clay pots fashioned into animals or ceramic pottery in a vibrant confetti of primary colors. Look for garden

STRAWBERRY JAR

Strawberry jars seem to hold everything *but* strawberries! These terra cotta jars with the little side pockets look terrific when planted with trailing herbs like thyme, savory or marjoram. But as attractive as strawberry jars are and no matter what you plant, watering evenly is a problem.

There is a method, though, to get water all the way from top to bottom. Here's how.

Before planting the jar, cut a length of 2- or 3-inch-diameter PVC pipe long enough to reach within 2 inches of the bottom of the strawberry jar. Drill 3/8-inch holes in the sides of the pipe at the levels of each pocket opening. Hold the pipe in the center of the empty jar, and fill the jar with small gravel to the pipe's bottom. Now fill the rest of the

With the addition of a perforated pipe, all the plants in a strawberry jar can be kept evenly watered and flourishing.

container with moistened potting soil and plant your herbs. When you water, pour water into the pipe and let the water drip into the soil.

"junque," like empty gallon olive oil cans, antique watering cans, even old rubber boots.

Other choices for containers that make interesting homes for herbs include wine crates, whiskey barrels or large vertical drain tiles. For a novel rustic effect, hollow out a log or stump for planting a shaded, woodland herb garden.

Whatever you choose for a container, make sure it has adequate drainage holes. If necessary, drill holes in the bottom. If you don't want to risk breaking the container by drilling, plant the herb in a pot that fits inside, filling the bottom

of the outer container with 1 to 2 inches of small gravel.

Before planting in any previously planted container, scrub it well with a vinegar-and-water solution followed by a mild bleach-and-water solution. Finally, rinse thoroughly with plain water. This helps prevent soil-borne diseases from attacking your newly potted herbs.

Look for unusual objects, such as an antique wheelbarrow, to hold your herbs and create a focal point in the garden.

Don't overlook fun objects for planting herbs. Old shoes are often used, but here they've been re-created in concrete.

DESIGNING WITH CONTAINERS

There is an art in creating a container herb garden that makes an attractive visual statement, just as there is in a "regular" garden. By giving careful consideration to the size and shape of the pots, the texture and shape of the foliage of the herbs and the color of their leaves and flowers, you can develop an integrated design that dresses up the most mundane of settings.

When combining herbs or other plants in containers, don't forget to consider cultural compatibility—no planting of water-loving watercress with drought-loving cactus.

Your container herb garden might be just one large pot filled with a half-dozen herbs, or you may want to "decorate" an area with a number of herbs in pots.

For a flamboyant Southwestern look, consider 'Starbright' and 'Persian Carpet' zinnias and 'Super Chile' peppers planted in a bright red-glazed pot. Nearby is the bright green, frilly texture of curly parsley planted in a wide terra cotta pot. The richly variegated foliage of golden lemon thyme planted in a brilliant purple container highlights the fiesta-like atmosphere.

For a more serene effect, think about a patio surrounded with romantic plantings of pastel-hued, old-fashioned roses. Highlight the area with wooden Versailles planters filled with green-and-white pineapple mint, the pebbly gray leaves of garden sage and the bright green leaves of lemon balm.

A formal container garden might be designed with a grouping of miniature or standard herbal topiaries in graceful stone or cast iron planters etched with classic relief. A possibility for an informal country look is to plant herbs in baskets.

A well-used stepladder becomes a piece of functional sculpture when filled with pots of herbs. Plus, this allows plenty of air circulation for the plants.

Combining pots of herbs with whimsical elements (such as this antique pushcart) brings your own personality into the garden.

Adding pots of herbs along the edge of the garden, as well as inside a bed or border, brings depth and dimension.

An old iron kettle not only serves as a container for an assortment of herbs, but when set into the groundcover makes the area much more interesting.

Personalize your container grouping design by incorporating interesting elements. These might be found objects relating to gardening or old garden ornaments or artifacts. Look for concrete orbs and pineapples, colorful metallic gazing globes, a collection of antique trowels or watering cans, marble busts, sundials, birdfeeders, sculpted animals or baskets of different materials.

In container groupings, place smaller pots at different levels to heighten interest. Draft worn old benches, tables or chairs, used "as is," for plant stands. Or, give them new life with a colorful coat of paint. This is an excellent way to recycle old furniture for use in the garden. A stepped metal plant stand lined with pots of the most-used culinary herbs makes both a handy and an ornamental object when situated next to an outdoor dining table on the patio or terrace.

Container herbs make an excellent focal point in the garden, either by themselves or complementing another element. Explore your yard for places to improve with a collection of herbs in containers. For example, you might provide design interest at the entry of the house by tucking a group of potted herbs (best planted in groups of three) in or near the foundation planting or placed in a garden border with flowers and foliage of complementary colors and textures. Herbs all of the same genus and species make an outstanding feature when lined up in a row, soldier-style, along the side of the driveway or against a blank wall on the side of the house. A large pot of lemon grass or a grand topiary placed beside a water garden adds complexity and height.

Wooden baskets filled with herbs make dramatic "finials" to the stone posts, while the pots on the steps and terrace soften the hard look of the stone.

A single, perfectly trained bay tree topiary in a traditional Versailles planter makes a dramatic accent in the garden.

PLANT COMBINATIONS

Bring together your favorite culinary herbs, such as this collection of tarragon, parsley, sage, rosemary and thyme, then accent them with brilliantly colored flowers such as these fall chrysanthemums.

Once your eyes get in the habit of considering the form, foliage, color and texture of herbs, you'll envision pleasing combinations endlessly...and the design of container planting becomes more and more rewarding.

Theme gardens are fun to create in containers. This might be a collection of herbs with variegated foliage, herbs with flowers of one color, lemon-scented herbs surrounding a dwarf lemon tree or a grouping of herbs native to the Mediterranean. Consider combining herbs specific to a particular cuisine, such as Mexican, Italian, French, Chinese,

Japanese or Southeast Asian. For instance, in a Mexican- or Southwestern-theme planter, combine sprawling Cuban oregano (with its picoteed, white-banded leaves), the upright, narrow-leaved Mexican tarragon, a hot pepper plant and pungent-scented cilantro.

One of the best choices among herbs to grow in pots are the mints. A pot is the perfect place for them because of their invasive growing habit. Try placing a large pot of your favorite mints just outside the kitchen door so that it will be convenient to snip a sprig or two for brightening up a dish or brewing a cup of tea.

Scented geraniums are among the best herbs for a container collection because they are not frost-hardy and must be brought indoors during the winter. Plus, they have a marvelous range of

Here's a bright idea for the garden. Set off a variegated sage with a dark container placed amid yellow pansies and calendulas.

Herbs planted together in a container should have similar growing requirements. This planter combines herbs that tolerate semi-shade—curly parsley, chervil, tarragon and sweet woodruff.

low, purple and white violas, for a lovely little salad bowl container.

In the heat of midsummer, a planting of sweet basil, French tarragon and chives, centered with tall, feathery fennel, provides a tasty combination to have in a container near the grill for last minute additions to food.

Play with textures and colors, combining similar or contrasting ones. A dramatic punctuation in the garden might be a grouping of grassy herbs such as lemon grass, buffalo grass and both the green and variegated forms of society garlic. The woolly gray, tongue-shaped leaves of lamb's-ears paired with the contrasting crinkled pur-

Consider size, shape, texture and color when combining herbs in containers. This variegated mint really brightens this planter, while the creeping rosemary softens the edges.

ple leaves of purple perilla is bold and effective.

A beautiful, healthy vegetable planted in a pot and surrounded by a complementary culinary herb makes a charming twosome. For instance, a fat, crinkly-leaved savoy cabbage set in a nest of trailing caraway thyme makes an appealing combination. A shallow terra cotta pot of Bibb lettuce planted with cascading nasturtiums resembles a large-petalled green flower—and supplies salad ingredients!

fragrances such as rose, lemon, apricot, apple or mint, to name only a few.

Winter savory (with its creeping stems and dark green leaves) contrasts with upright, pink-flowered summer savory and the light green, lacy leaves of chervil. They make an appealing trio planted together in a container. The large-leaved 'Berggarten' sage planted with sweet marjoram and French thyme offers a handsome Mediterranean threesome. Creeping rosemary planted with 'Munstead' lavender and orange balsam thyme is a sensory delight with its textures and fragrances.

Combine an assortment of plants that all thrive in cool weather such as chervil planted with an assortment of lettuces and the edible flowers of calendula, Johnny-jump-ups and yel-

Play with color in the garden, moving containers of herbs around to accent different flowers. Here, the pink in the tricolor sage leaves blends with the pink flowers of the rose and the society garlic. The yellow-variegated sage blends in the with yellow flowers across the path.

CARING FOR CONTAINER PLANTINGS

Unlike herbs planted in the ground, container-grown herbs are entirely dependent on the gardener for *all* their needs. Roots can't forage endlessly in the soil for nutrition as they do in the ground; therefore, they must be fertilized more often. And with the plant roots above ground level, they need protection from the extremes of cold and heat.

Container-grown herbs also have increased watering needs. Herbs with their roots in garden soil can survive a certain amount of drought; not so for those grown in containers, where the soil dries out faster. Conversely, the soil mix must drain quickly so the roots don't become waterlogged.

Fortunately, it is easy to supply a healthy environment for container-grown herbs.

Good drainage is perhaps the most important factor for growing herbs. The plants are very forgiving, but the one thing they do not tolerate is soggy, non-draining soil, which will certainly cause root rot. Therefore, soil choice for the container garden is paramount. The growing medium should provide fast water drainage and, at the same time, have the capability to provide adequate moisture, air and nutrients.

Fortunately, the soilless mixes readily available at nurseries and garden centers provide all of these attributes except nutrients. The formulas are usually combinations of peat mixed with perlite and/or vermiculite. Before filling the containers, first mix in a generous cupful of

Good drainage and air circulation is just as important for container-grown herbs as it is for those planted in the garden.

An advantage of growing herbs in containers is that you can move them to follow the sun. Prevent back pain by placing large pots on a caster-wheeled plant stand.

stands add flexibility to your garden of container herbs so that you can move the pots as seasonal light patterns shift or the sun's rays become too hot. It's fun to have the option to continually create changes in the garden, just as you do with household furniture and interior decor.

Expect to water the container herb garden not by the calendar but by the finger test. If the top inch or so of soil is dry, then by all means soak the containers thoroughly. During hot spells, or for plants in a constantly

sunny location, test the soil daily. Use a watering can with a sprinkler hose or a hose fitted with a water-breaker or soft-flow nozzle so that the force of the water doesn't splash the soil out of the pot or disturb the plant roots. When the soil stops bubbling and water freely runs out the drainage holes, you know the soil is saturated.

Water herbs early in the morning instead of in the evening, as wet leaves in the evening foster mildew and other disease organisms. The lightweight pebbles of white perlite will rise to the top of the soil when watered, causing a rather messy appearance. Cover the top of the soil with a layer of smooth river rocks, shredded bark, or other mulch. This also helps keep the soil moist and cool.

Herbs grown in containers thrive on a constant supply of nutrients given in small but regular feedings, such as with a mixture of fish emulsion and seaweed or 20-20-20 liquid fertilizer mixed at half strength, every 10 days to two weeks.

dehydrated cow manure (worm or cricket castings are alternatives) and a scant 1/4-cup of rock or collodial phosphate to each bushel of potting mix. Alternatively, use a commercially available complete organic or natural fertilizer at the manufacturer's recommended rate. You could mix in moisture-retaining polymer granules at this time, too. Finally, moisten the potting mix thoroughly with warm water.

To prepare a container for planting, cover the drainage holes in the container with mesh screening, which deters sow bugs and slugs. Fill the pots with the moistened potting mix to within 1 inch of the top of the pot.

Elevate containers on bricks or caster-wheeled plant stands to create good air circulation around them. The movable

Keep containers of herbs adequately watered, soaking the soil thoroughly. At least once a month, add a water-soluble fertilizer such as fish emulsion.

HERBS INDOORS

The possibility of harvesting your own fresh herbs indoors in winter is a great motivator for making the extra effort to successfully grow them.

Once you get used to the exceptional flavor of fresh, home-grown herbs, the winter months can seem longer than ever. How wonderful it would be to have that taste year-round! With just a little effort, it really is possible to grow some of your favorite culinary herbs indoors.

There are several different ways to approach growing herbs indoors. First, of course, is to bring all those herbs already growing in containers outdoors into the house in the autumn. You'll especially want to bring in the tender potted herbs, such as scented geraniums, bay, lemon verbena or rosemary.

An alternative is to either buy new, young plants in the autumn or start them yourself from seed or cuttings. The best herbs to grow from seed indoors include basil, chervil, cilantro, dill ('Fernleaf' is best), parsley, marjoram and summer savory. For cuttings, try basil, mint, oregano, pineapple sage, rosemary, sage, scented geraniums and thyme.

Another possibility is to dig up and pot plants from the garden. The herbs that you are most likely to have success with are chives, garlic chives, Greek oregano, lavender, any of the mints, rosemary, sage, scented geranium, summer savory, marjoram, French tarragon and thyme. Some people have success bringing them directly indoors, while others give them a cold treatment first. To do this, sink the pot in the ground up to the rim. After three or four hard frosts, bring the pot indoors.

Light

Herbs indoors need the brightest light possible, such as that from an unobstructed south-facing window. An east- or west-facing window might work, especially if there are no trees or other obstructions. Rotate them a quarter turn every week so that all sides receive light.

If you don't have that kind of situation, consider using a fluorescent or high-intensity grow light. Place the light source about a foot above the plants. Consider installing an automatic timer so that the light turns on in the morning and off at night, or in any 12-hour interval you choose.

Temperature and Humidity

Most of our favorite culinary herbs grow best with daytime temperatures indoors of 60 to 70°F. At night, a 10-degree drop is ideal. Indoor air during the winter is notorious for being woefully dry, which is unhealthy for both people and plants. Consider installing a

Many gardeners like to bring tender perennial herbs, like the bay, rosemary and lemon grass shown here, indoors in winter to keep them growing year after year.

Bright sunlight, daytime temperatures between 60 and 70°F and a 10-degree temperature drop at night make ideal conditions for growing most herbs indoors.

Grow herbs under fluorescent growlights if you don't have a sunny enough window. Let the top of the soil dry out slightly between thorough waterings.

humidifier on your furnace or placing a room humidifier near your herbs. You can also place the pots on trays filled with pebbles and water; just make sure the pots do not sit in the water.

Water

The water requirements of herbs grown indoors vary from herb to herb. Basil, chervil, mint and parsley do best with the potting soil kept evenly moist. Let rosemary and lavender dry out slightly between waterings. When in doubt, err on the side of letting the top $^1/_2$ inch of the soil dry out before watering.

Fertilizer

Adjust the feeding schedule in winter to the light level. If the light is not bright and the herbs are not actively growing, do not fertilize at all until spring. For a bright-light situation (either natural or artificial) where the herbs continue to send out new growth, fertilize monthly with a fertilizer formulated for indoor plants; use it according to the manufacturer's directions.

Pests

Herbs are much more susceptible to pests indoors. Aphids, whiteflies, mealybugs and scale are the most frequent culprits. Before bringing outdoor plants inside, spray them with food-safe horticultural soap. Maintaining a humid atmosphere and washing the foliage thoroughly once a week will often be enough to keep pests at bay. If pests do appear, control them with a food-safe horticultural soap spray. To prevent fungal diseases, make sure air flows freely around plants; a small fan placed nearby ensures this.

Harvesting

If you've gone to this much trouble, surely you don't need to be encouraged to add herbs to all your cooking during the winter. Harvesting helps keep each plant compact and well-shaped. To have enough fresh young foliage, especially of the seed-grown herbs, start a new planting every month or so.

In the Spring

When spring arrives, harden off the overwintered herbs just as you do with seedlings. Place them outdoors in a sheltered spot on warm, sunny days, bringing them in at night. Repeat for one to two weeks. When it seems that the last frost has occurred, move them once again to wherever you want in the landscape.

If you want houseplants, why not make them edible, especially if they are as delicious as this chocolate mint.

CHAPTER 5

USING THE HERBAL BOUNTY

The most rewarding aspect of growing culinary herbs, aside from the pleasure of their beauty and fragrance in the garden, is bringing them into the kitchen and your meals.

Throughout the growing season, you can gather herbs on a daily basis. Gather a bit of gently pungent garlic chives for a stir-fry, some clove-scented basil for sprinkling on slices of just-picked tomatoes or a sprig of mint for your iced tea. Then there is the grand end-of-season harvest for preserving herbs to extend their use year-round.

When your herbs are at rest in the garden, perhaps under a blanket of snow in cold climates or just having a seasonal nap in warmer regions, they still generously offer their unique flavors in the kitchen. Besides simply drying your herbs, you can create a wide assortment of herbal treats that will play a role in your cooking from appetizers to desserts.

And soon you'll find yourself making, using and sharing your own homemade herbal vinegars, butters, blends, sugars, jellies and other flavorful items.

USING HERBS IN THE KITCHEN

A soothing cup of hot herb tea is the reward in winter for taking the time to dry herbs during the growing season.

The motto of The Herb Society of America is "For Use and Delight." Nowhere is this phrase better applied than on daily trips to your own herb garden, for both the utilitarian

and pleasurable aspects of culinary herbs are never-ending.

On a morning trip to the garden you might gather freshly snipped chives or tarragon—or both—for a breakfast omelet. A leaf or two of sage, chopped fine, enhances biscuit batter, either homemade or a store-bought mix. Or, use a sprig of rosemary in a similar manner to spark a box of commercial corn-bread mix.

A stroll through the herb garden just before lunchtime might produce a fresh lettuce salad jazzed up with spicy nasturtium leaves and garnished with sun-shine-colored calendula petals. Or, a large handful of sorrel might make its way into a chilled potato-and-sorrel soup.

In the late afternoon, when you are perhaps just leaving the garden after a day's work there, a few sprigs of mint infused in a refreshing cup of honey-sweetened mint tea rewards your travails. Or, if so inclined, transform that mint into a mint julep instead! A few little radish-and-

Herbs even lend themselves to desserts, whether for a rose-geranium cake, strawberry-mint shortcake, peach-basil pie or viola parfait.

burnet sandwiches would taste great, too.

On the last daily trip to the garden just before dinner, gather some fennel or dill to perfume a fillet of salmon. The slender leaves of Mexican tarragon lend a pot of steamed green beans a unique anise flavor. For dessert, sprinkle some minced cinnamon basil over sliced fresh peaches.

When you grow herbs and use them daily in the kitchen, you'll become aware of the subtle changes that happen with the foods emanating from your kitchen. The "suspicion" of herb flavor is the desired goal in

What could be more satisfying than a homemade pizza using fresh vegetables and herbs from your own garden?

Edible herbal flowers, such as those of bergamot, rose, borage and calendula, turn a dessert of fresh blackberries into a work of art.

cooking with herbs. You want to give foods complexity without dominating them with the the taste of any particular herb. The following are some useful tips when cooking with herbs:

- Add robust herbs such as bay, oregano, thyme, rosemary or sage, at the beginning of cooking a long-simmering dish. In general, use no more than two robust herbs in a dish. Add the more delicate-tasting herbs, such as basil, chervil, chives and dill, toward the end of cooking.
- When using dried herbs, crush them between your fingers in the palm of your hand before adding them to the pot. This helps release their essential oils (and makes you feel good as you inhale the fragrance of the herbs). With dried rosemary, chop it finely, as the leaves tend to be tough.
- A guideline for substituting dried herbs for fresh ones is to use one-third to one-half as much dried as fresh. For example, with a recipe calling for 1 tablespoon fresh herb, substitute 1 to 1^1/$_2$ teaspoons dried. The exceptions are rosemary and sage; with these, use one-quarter as much dried as fresh.
- When increasing recipes, do not double the amount of herbs used. Increase them only by one-and-a-half.
- When using herb seeds (such as dill, coriander or fennel) in a vinaigrette dressing, soak them first in vinegar to soften them and release their flavor.

- Soak dried herbs for 30 minutes in the stock, wine, brandy or other liquid to be used in a recipe.
- Add fresh herbs to the cooking water when steaming vegetables, then sprinkle some of the same herb, minced, over the vegetables just before serving.
- Until you become familiar with an herb, add it in small amounts, tasting until the flavor suits you. In fact, cooking to the *cook's* taste is what personalizes your own herb cooking.

Herbs partner well with all kinds of breads, muffins, biscuits or scones. Simply choose an herb and add it to your favorite recipe.

Experiment with herbs in all kinds of foods—soups, marinades for grilled foods, cookie bars or any of your favorite dishes.

GATHERING, STORING & FREEZING FRESH HERBS

Plan on utilizing edible flowers as soon as possible after picking them. If necessary you can briefly store them between layers of paper towels in an airtight container in the refrigerator.

The flavor oils in herbs are at their highest in early morning after the dew has dried, but don't hesitate to gather at any time of day because the flavor of herbs always makes food taste better.

Gathering Herbs

Gather a sprig of this or that from the garden for daily cooking at any time of day. When you're collecting herbs in quantity, especially for preserving, the ideal time to gather them is in the early morning, as that is when they are at their peak of flavor. Harvest after the dew has evaporated but before the sun becomes hot. During the heat of the day, the aromatic and flavorful essential oils in the leaves of the herbs diminish as their moisture escapes into the atmosphere.

When gathering a few herbs for cooking, snip 2 or 3 inches of the young stem tips, as well as older and larger leaves along the stems. Regularly gathering herbs is not only useful in the kitchen, but the constant little prunings promote lush and healthy new growth.

Normally you can take at least several major harvests from your herbs each season. Plants may be cut back by one-third during mid-season just before flowering. After this harvest, lightly work compost or fertilizer into the soil around the plant to ensure a healthy second growth. There will be another harvest in late summer or fall.

In cold climates, the last harvest of perennial herbs is best taken no later than one month before the first frost. This prevents the plant from being weakened before winter. At the end of the growing season, simply cut annual herbs to the ground.

The last major harvest of the season from your herb garden is usually best done a month before the first frost for perennials or right up to the first frost for annuals.

Storing Fresh Herbs

Storage methods for fresh-cut herbs vary according to the herb. For example, chervil, cilantro, dill or parsley stay fresh for a week or so if placed in a wide-mouth jar or glass of water and covered with a plastic sandwich bag. They will last longer if kept in the refrigerator. Basil, however, turns an unappetizing black with this treatment. Instead, treat it as a bouquet of flowers. No plastic bag for basil, just stand it in a glass of water

on a sunny windowsill. It will stay fresh for a week or more—if you can resist using it in cooking for that long!

Another way to keep herbs fresh is to wrap them in damp paper towels, then place them in zippered plastic bags. Kept in the vegetable compartment of the refrigerator, the herbs last up to several weeks. Cilantro stays fresh best by pulling up the young plants and leaving the roots intact until ready to use.

Freezing Herbs

Freezing herbs is a good method to use for basil, chervil, chives, cilantro, dill, lemon balm, lovage, mint, parsley, sage, sorrel, sweet cicely or tarragon. Mix 2 cups of finely chopped herbs with 1 cup water. Or, swirl the leaves and water in a blender. Pour the mixture into ice-cube trays. When frozen, unmold the cubes and store in a sturdy zippered plastic bag. Label it with the name of the herb and the date. When you want to flavor a dish with the herb, simply add one or two of the frozen cubes.

Create frozen herb cubes to capture that fresh herb taste for use at other times of year. Just drop a cube into a dish you're cooking.

A variation on this technique is to use olive or canola oil instead of water in the same proportions. Either freeze as cubes or in an airtight container, dipping out a spoonful as needed.

Another method of freezing herbs is to place washed and dried leaves in small plastic freezer bags, then label, date and freeze. When ready to use, just break off pieces of the frozen clusters. The texture and color may suffer, but they retain their flavor for about six months.

After harvesting fresh herbs, they can be kept available for use for several days, either in jars of water or loosely wrapped in damp paper towels placed in plastic bags in the refrigerator.

Freeze individual basil leaves by washing, drying on a towel and then placing in small plastic freezer bags. Be sure to label and date the package.

DRYING HERBS

When drying herbs in bundles, hang them upside down. Be sure to choose a dark, dry and well-ventilated room so that the herbs dry quickly and retain their flavor oils.

Preserving herbs by drying them is the most popular and easiest method of capturing their essential flavor oils. A cache of bright green, crispy herbs in glass bottles lined up on a cupboard shelf is a rewarding sight to the gardener-cook, especially when the contents are home-grown.

The case for having a supply of dried herbs in the kitchen is underscored in winter when the garden is frozen solid under a blanket of snow, but the herbs are at hand for any last-minute cooking situations.

In many herb garden books, one inevitably comes across the picturesque colonial image of herbs hung to dry from kitchen rafters. These are fine for decor, but there are less dusty methods of drying herbs for culinary use.

Microwave Drying

Now that the microwave oven is a regular feature in contemporary kitchens, this modern-day method for drying herbs provides crisp, bright green leaves in just minutes. It's easy and convenient. Quickly rinse the herbs, then pat them thoroughly dry with a paper towel or spin them dry in a salad spinner. Place the stems side by side in a single layer between two sheets of paper towels in the microwave oven. Heat on high power in increments of one minute until the herbs are parchment dry. Most herbs dry in about 3 to 4 minutes.

Gently strip the dried leaves from the stems and place them whole in small, airtight, clean, wide-mouth glass bottles. Fill extra bottles for family and friends. A bottle or two of beautifully labeled herbs makes a perfect host or hostess gift.

After filling the bottles, label and date, then store the herbs in a cool, dark place. As attractive as bottles of herbs perched on a shelf over the kitchen stove might be, light and heat diminish this treasure trove from the garden. Dried herbs maintain flavor for one year, perfect for using them up before next summer's harvest, when the process begins anew.

Air Drying

Some herb gardeners feel that the microwave method of drying herbs, however speedy, may rob the leaves of too much essential oil. One alternative is to dry herbs in a food dehydrator. For gardeners who prefer a more "old-fashioned" way, there are three other time-honored methods of drying herbs.

With the first one, you gather small bunches of herb branches and tie them into bundles with string. Place them with the tip ends down in a brown paper bag, with the

With experience, you'll be able to tell when it's time to harvest the seed heads of herbs such as dill. The seeds must be ripe but harvested before they begin to fall.

stem ends extending several inches over the top. Close the bag around the bouquet and secure with string, leaving a loop for hanging. Suspend the bag, clothesline fashion, on a cord in a dry, well-ventilated room. Depending on the humidty, the herbs should be dry in about a week to 10 days. Gently strip the whole leaves from the stems. Place them in clean glass jars and label.

A second method for drying herbs is to crisp them in the kitchen oven. Position the herbs, uncrowded, in a single layer on a cookie sheet lined with parchment paper. Place in a pre-heated 150°F oven with the door ajar. The herbs are usually dry in 30 minutes to several hours. Allow the herbs to cool, then strip the stems of the leaves and proceed with bottling and labeling.

The third traditional method is to dry herbs on fine-mesh screens, suspended or supported so that there is good air circulation all around. Drying time depends on the humidity and the herb, so check the herbs' progress daily.

One More Technique

A unique and ever-so-easy method of drying small amounts of herb was discovered by herb authority, gardener and cook Madalene Hill of Texas. Utilizing a frost-free refrigerator, place herb leaves, uncovered, on a plate set on a refrigerator shelf. In about five to six days, the herbs are crisp and dry. Whole stems dry in one week. Bring the herbs to room temperature, then package in glass jars.

Whatever method you choose to dry herbs, tie the remaining dried stems into aromatic little bundles. Keep these on the hearth for throwing onto winter fires while snow or cold weather keeps you indoors.

Drying Tips

1 Tie herb stems together with a rubber band so that as the stems dry and shrink, the bundle is still held securely together.

3 Another way to dry herbs: spread them out on a screen placed in a well-ventilated location or in an oven set to 150°F.

2 To make sure the herbs don't get dusty or to catch seeds as they fall, tie an upside-down bundle in a paper bag with holes cut out for ventilation.

4 When the leaves are crispy-dry like cereal, gently strip them from the stems over a clean sheet of paper.

5 Lift the paper and carefully pour the herbs into a clean, dry container. The less you crush the leaves, the more flavor they retain.

6 Gently shake or rub dried seeds over a paper bag to catch them. If they don't come loose easily, place the stems upside down in the bag until they dry more.

HERB VINEGARS

Herb vinegars are incredibly easy to make, and they add a new dimension of flavor to all kinds of foods beyond salads. To give a bottle of herb vinegar as a gift, add an herb sprig to the already-flavored vinegar and top with a rafia bow.

Vinegar is an ancient and universal accompaniment to food. When it is infused with the essences of various herbs, creativity in the kitchen reigns. Basil, rosemary, sage, dill or tarragon are particularly effective because of their savory pungency. Others, such as mint or lavender, lend more subtle taste and fragrance. Like the pleasure of observing little bottles of dried herbs from your own garden harvest, glistening, jewel-like bottles of vinegars adorning the pantry shelf are also joyful to behold by the gardener and cook.

White or red wine vinegars, sherry vinegar, apple cider vinegar or rice vinegar are all complementary carriers waiting to be transformed into a variety of pungent to delicate herb-flavored vinegars. The more assertive herbs (like oregano, garlic, rosemary or sage) marry well with red wine or sherry vinegars. The "lighter" herbs are best in white wine or rice vinegar. Apple cider vinegar works well with the full spectrum of herbs.

Purple basil imparts only a mild flavor to white wine or rice vinegar but colors it a lovely, rosy hue. The secret to making it more assertive is to also steep green sweet basil along with the purple. Use green and purple perillas in the same manner to flavor and color clear vinegars.

Experiment with various combinations of herbs to make your own signature house vinegar. For variety, add other flavorings—such as chili peppers, garlic, shallots, pearl onions, peppercorns or lemon or orange slices—to give an even more complex flavor to vinegars.

Herb vinegars are obvious choices for using in tart vinaigrettes, but there are many other ways to take advantage of their flavors. Try deglazing sautéed meat or chicken. Add them to marinades before grilling. Sprinkle them over cooked vegetables or add a spoonful to soup just before serving.

In midsummer or whenever herbs are about to flower is a good time to infuse them in vinegar. Don't be afraid, though, to experiment with making vinegars whenever you please. Gather one or more large handfuls of herbs. Wash and pat them dry with paper towels. Place them, stems and all, in a sterilized, wide-mouth jar. Fill the jar at least half full. Bruise the herbs with the back of a wooden spoon. Fill the jar with the vinegar of your choice, making sure the herbs are totally submerged. Cover the jar tightly with a non-reactive lid or secure a piece of plastic wrap with a rubber band. Set the jar in a cool, dark place.

In one week, taste the vinegar. If the strength suits you, strain the vinegar through a fine-meshed sieve lined with several layers of cheesecloth. Pour the strained vinegar into a sterilized glass jar with a non-reactive lid. Cover tightly. Store in cool, dark spot on the pantry shelf; it will keep for at least one year.

Resist the temptation to show off your pretty bottles of herb vinegars by putting them on a sunny windowsill where the light streams through. While it is indeed an artful display, light quickly dissipates the flavor.

Only use metal caps that are plastic lined, because vinegar corrodes metal. As tempting as it is to leave vinegar sitting out, the flavor is better retained when the bottles are stored in a dark, cool pantry.

HERB BUTTERS

Combining minced herbs with butter yields a special hint of flavor to steamed vegetables, baked potatoes, bread or rolls. To have some summer-fresh flavor in the middle of winter, store differently flavored butters in airtight containers in the freezer.

Herb butters are one of the most convenient methods of capturing the essential oils of various culinary herbs. You can make herb butters in amounts as small as a tablespoon. When you find one that particularly pleases you, then you can prepare larger amounts, form them into cylinders and slice off "coins" to add a dollop of flavor to foods whenever you want.

Herb butters are excellent for adding zip to cooked vegetables, especially corn-on-the-cob. Don't overlook how they can benefit pasta, rice or soup. And why not add some to scrambled eggs or omelettes? Or, make them the final touch for melting over grilled fish or chicken. A little ramekin or two of herb butter on the dining table always elicits praise when spread on rolls or crusty bread.

Making herb butters is a simple matter. A good ratio is 2 tablespoons of finely chopped herbs, either singly or in combination, to 1/2 cup softened sweet butter. When using rosemary, sage or oregano, use somewhat less. Add a teaspoon

Complement specific breads, rolls, scones or muffins with herb butters you tailor-make.

of lemon juice, if desired. Cream the butter and herbs with a spoon or mixer. Spoon the mixture onto a short length of wax paper, then roll the paper over the butter and roll back and forth to make a small "log" that is 1 1/2 to 2 inches in diameter. Twist the ends of the paper, label, and store in the refrigerator for up to two weeks. These herb butter logs also keep in the freezer for several months.

One favorite of the classic chef's "compound butters" (as they are known in the restaurant trade) is maitre d'hotel butter. This is a fancy term for a mixture of chervil, parsley, chives and tarragon in equal amounts, a bit of lemon juice and a pinch of salt.

Other flavorings to combine with herb butters include garlic, shallots (for a mild onion flavor), mustard, horseradish, paprika, pimiento or nuts such as pistachios, hazelnuts or almonds. Liqueurs, such as Grand Marnier or Framboise, added to herb butters in small quantities, lend a unique flavor. Adding to fruit preserves is another possibility.

Make one of the prettiest herb butters by chopping a confetti of edible flowers and allowing their floral flavor to infuse the butter. The edible flowers of basil, chives, dill, oregano or rosemary subtly mimic the flavor of the leaves. Try other edible flowers too. Your imagination is your guide for creating endless combinations of tasty herb butters.

HERB BLENDS

Herb blends offer a quick and easy way to add flavor to foods without calories, fat or salt. Use your own home-dried herbs, which will taste better than store-bought. Whether you combine your favorite herbs or use some of the accompanying recipes, get in the habit of using them every day. And don't forget to make some for gifts.

Mediterranean Herb Blend
2 tablespoons dried rosemary
2 tablespoons dried parsley
2 tablespoons dried summer savory
2 tablespoons dried marjoram
1 tablespoon garlic powder
1 tablespoon onion powder

Fish Blend
1/4 cup dried dill
2 tablespoons dried parsley
2 tablespoons dried lemon basil
2 tablespoons dried lemon balm
2 tablespoons dried garlic chives

Soup Seasoning Blend
3 tablespoons dried parsley
1 tablespoon dried thyme
1 tablespoon dried chervil
1 tablespoon dried basil
1 tablespoon dried marjoram
1 tablespoon dried lovage
1 teaspoon dried lemon zest

Herbal Salad Dressing Mix
2 tablespoons dried chervil
1 tablespoon dried basil
1 teaspoon dried thyme
1 teaspoon dried lovage
1 teaspoon dried tarragon
1 teaspoon dried dill
1/2 teaspoon paprika
1/4 teaspoon ground black pepper

Poultry Seasoning
1/4 cup dried parsley
2 tablespoons dried sage
1 tablespoon dried summer savory
1 tablespoon dried rosemary
1 tablespoon dried lovage
1 tablespoon dried marjoram

Herb blends, with or without salt, are easy to make at home with dried herbs from the garden. Besides being less expensive than store-bought combinations, the herbs in homemade versions are your own choice. Some of the herbs that you may want to include as a base in herb blends are parsley, marjoram and thyme.

To make an herb blend, finely crush the dried herbs and combine thoroughly. If desired, mix with an equal amount or less of ground sea salt. Besides the culinary herbs, there are a number of other possible additions, including mild or hot paprika, garlic powder or granules, onion powder or granules, celery seeds, sesame seeds or curry powder. Once you have the combination completed, bottle in clean glass jars, cap tightly and label. Store on a cool, dark shelf.

Herbes de Provence Blend
3 tablespoons dried thyme
2 tablespoons dried marjoram
2 tablespoons dried summer savory
2 teaspoons dried rosemary
1 teaspoon fennel seeds
1 teaspoon dried lavender flowers
1/2 teaspoon dried sage

HERB CHEESES

Whether as part of an appetizer tray for a party or your own private midnight snack, be sure to make some cream cheese or homemade yogurt cheese that bursts with the flavor of fresh herbs. Besides the combinations suggested here, don't be afraid to try mixtures of your own favorite herbs.

Dessert Herb Cheese

A cheese course as dessert is becoming popular again. This non-fat version brings the goodness of yogurt cheese enhanced with the brightness of lemon and the soothing flavor of mint. Spread it on thin cookies such as ginger snaps, or on toasted slices of a sweet quick bread. Include some fresh fruit and you have a luxurious but healthy dessert.

1 tablespoon fresh spearmint
1 tablespoon lemon balm
1 tablespoon lemon basil
8 ounces homemade non-fat
    lemon- or vanilla-yogurt cheese

Combine all ingredients in a food processor. Blend until smooth and chill.

Savory Herb Cheese

Adding minced herbs to fresh cheeses such as cream cheese, goat cheese or homemade yogurt cheese, creates a luscious appetizer, party food or snack. Choose your own favorite herbs or try this combination, which resembles an expensive store-bought one.

1 clove garlic
1 tablespoon fresh parsley
1 teaspoon fresh dill
1 teaspoon fresh basil
1 teaspoon fresh marjoram
1 teaspoon fresh chives
1 teaspoon fresh thyme
$^1/_4$ teaspoon salt
$^1/_8$ teaspoon freshly ground black
    pepper
8 ounces cream cheese, goat
    cheese or homemade yogurt
    cheese, at room temperature

Combine all ingredients in a food processor. Process until smooth. Chill and serve with crackers.

HOMEMADE YOGURT CHEESE

With the consistency of cream cheese, yogurt cheese is made by straining the whey from yogurt. There are commercially available strainers for this, but you can create one by lining a large strainer or colander with several layers of cheesecloth. Place this over a bowl and fill with 32 ounces of yogurt. Let it drain for several hours. Remove the cheese from the strainer and store in the refrigerator. You can use the whey for baking.

This cheese is best made from a yogurt that does not contain gelatin. The healthiest version uses plain, non-fat yogurt. For a dessert cheese, try vanilla or lemon yogurt.

Even cheesecake can be good for you if made from homemade yogurt cheese flavored with herbs. And it can be a showstopping dessert when decorated with herb flowers like borage, bergamot petals, white violets and calendula.

SWEET WAYS TO PRESERVE HERBS

Crystallized Leaves and Flowers

For beautiful and edible decorations on cakes and pastries, nothing compares to crystallized viola flowers, rose petals or mint leaves. Just brush a little egg white all over each flower, petal or leaf and dip each one into superfine or powdered sugar. Place on wax paper to dry. After the sugar has dried, store in an airtight container. If using raw egg whites is a concern, substitute the powdered egg white available at groceries, reconstituting it as directed on the package.

Herb Sugars

One of the delightful treats of growing the "sweet herbs" is to flavor sugar. The leaves of herbs such as scented geraniums, lemon verbena or mint, and the flowers or petals of lavender, dianthus or roses easily and quickly scent and flavor sugar. Add the sugar to hot or iced tea or lemonade, or use them in preparing uncooked desserts.

Simply layer the leaves or flowers with sugar in an airtight container. Stir every day to prevent clumping. Once the sugar stays dry and loose, remove the leaves or flowers before they start to crumble.

Herb Syrups

Another sweet pleasure from herbs is to capture their flavor in a sugar syrup. Pour these syrups over fruit, bread pudding, rice pudding, pound cake or ice cream. Or, use the syrup to make ice cream, sorbet, custard or other desserts. Consider such herbs as anise hyssop, basil, dianthus, lavender, lemon grass, lemon verbena, any of the mints or scented geraniums or roses.

An array of herb jellies, made with different juices and herbs, are delightful to have on hand. Use them on morning toast or to give as gifts.

Make a simple syrup by dissolving 1 cup sugar in 1 cup water in a heavy saucepan: bring to boil and cook, stirring, until the sugar dissolves. Reduce the heat and add 1 cup fresh herb flowers or leaves. Simmer, partially covered, for 30 minutes. Pour through a strainer. Cool slightly. Put into an airtight container and store in the refrigerator.

Herb Jellies

Herb jellies are the cook's signature to have on hand for spreading on morning toast, serving with crackers and cream cheese, or using as a sauce for

To create herb sugar, layer herb leaves or flower petals with sugar. Stir every day, and remove the herbs before they crumble.

game, meat or poultry dishes. Made with either a single herb or a complementary combination of herbs, they are a delight on your own pantry shelf as well as cherished tokens to share with friends.

You can make herb jelly with apple juice as the base, in which case no pectin is needed. If another juice, wine or water is used, then you'll have to add either powdered or liquid pectin.

The basic procedure for herb jelly is to infuse the liquid with one or more herbs, then proceed with the jelly-making process. To make the infusion, wash and dry 1 cup of fresh herb leaves. Combine the herbs with the juice, water or wine in a saucepan and bring to a boil. Remove from heat and cover. Let steep for 30 minutes, then strain. If desired, substitute $^1/_2$ cup dried herbs for the fresh.

Some of the possible combinations include:
- Cranberry juice and rosemary
- Apple juice and sage
- Pink grapefruit juice with fennel, tarragon and chervil
- Cherry juice with lavender flowers

- Peach juice with cinnamon basil
- Orange juice with angelica and sweet cicely
- Riesling wine with sweet woodruff
- Rose wine with rose petals
- Red grape juice with hyssop
- White grape juice with thyme
- White wine with tarragon

Herb Jelly with Apple Juice

4 cups apple juice
1 cup fresh herb leaves or flowers
3 cups sugar
$^1/_2$ teaspoon butter or margarine

Make the herb infusion as described. Put the strained infusion in a heavy saucepan, put on high heat and bring to a rolling boil. Stir in sugar and butter or margarine. Stirring constantly, bring back to a rolling boil and boil for about 10 minutes or until 222°F on a candy thermometer. Remove from heat, skim, then fill jars. Proceed with standard directions for boiling-water method of preserving (following).

Herb Jelly with Powdered Pectin

3 cups fruit juice, water or wine
1 cup fresh herb leaves or flowers
1 tablespoon lemon juice or vinegar
1 package (1$^3/_4$ ounces) powdered pectin
$^1/_2$ teaspoon butter or margarine
4 cups sugar

Make the herb infusion as decribed. Put the strained infusion in a heavy saucepan with the lemon juice or vinegar, pectin and butter or margarine. Put on high heat and, stirring constantly, bring to a full rolling boil. Stir in sugar. Continuing to stir, return to a full boil and boil for one minute. Remove from heat, skim, then fill jars. Proceed with standard directions for boiling-water method of preserving (following).

Herb Jelly with Liquid Pectin

1$^1/_2$ cups juice, water or wine
1 cup fresh herb leaves or petals
3$^1/_2$ cups sugar
$^1/_2$ cup vinegar
$^1/_4$ teaspoon butter or margarine
1 pouch (3 ounces) liquid pectin

Make the herb infusion as decribed. Put the strained infusion in a heavy saucepan with the sugar, vinegar, and butter or margarine. Put on high heat and, stirring constantly, bring to a full rolling boil. Stir in pectin and, stirring constantly, return to a full rolling boil, continuing to boil for one minute. Remove from heat, skim, then fill jars. Proceed with standard directions for boiling-water method of preserving.

Standard Directions for Boiling-Water Method of Preserving

Pour the prepared jelly into a clean and hot half-pint jar, leaving $^1/_4$-inch space at the top. Wipe the rims, put on two-piece lids and fasten the screw bands. Put the jars on a rack in a deep kettle half full of boiling water. Add more boiling water, if necessary, to cover the lids by 2 inches. Cover the pot, bring to a hard boil for 10 minutes, lowering heat if necessary. Remove the jars from the boiling water. Cool, remove bands, label and store.

Mint jelly traditionally accompanies roast lamb.

◊ CHAPTER 6 ◊
CULINARY HERBS A TO Z

Here are all the favorite culinary herbs, organized alphabetically by common name, with the botanical name also given. Using the botanical name when you buy herbs means that you're most likely getting the exact plant you want.

For each herb, there is some history and folklore, as well as ways that it is used in cooking around the world. You'll find suggestions as to the foods that the herbs can be used in or with, as well as other ways to use them.

Then there's lots of gardening information about each plant, including whether it is an annual, biennial, perennial, vine, shrub or tree. To help you use the plants in the landscape, the size and description of the leaves and flowers is given, as well as where the herb is native. Plus, you'll find suggestions of related plants you might want to grow. Most importantly, details about hardiness, light, soil, planting, propagation and care needs are presented in detail. You'll also learn when to harvest and how to preserve each herb. We've also included a recipe with each herb! And don't be afraid to experiment when cooking with herbs.

There are lots more uses for the herbs than can fit in this book. There's always more to learn about herbs, to say nothing of gardening and cooking. The goal of these herb profiles is to ensure your success and open doors for continuing to grow, use and enjoy herbs for years to come.

HOW TO USE THIS SECTION

Culinary herbs represent a true potpourri, so to speak, of the gardening world. The herbs we love to grow—and then use to flavor our food with such wonderful hints and tastes—come from all corners of the globe. As such, herbs originate from a wide variety of plant families.

What does this mean to the gardener? Simply, that all herbs are not alike. Just as each herb has its own unique flavor and uses, it needs special conditions and care to grow and thrive before it can even get to your kitchen.

That's what this encyclopedia of herbs is all about—giving you the techniques, insights and tips you need to identify, grow, care for, harvest and use each culinary herb. You'll even find a wonderful recipe for each one.

To help simplify your decisions on which herbs you can grow where within your own gardening scheme, we devised the simple system explained below. Just look for the keys with each herb and you'll have, at a glance, the basic information you need to know about growing that herb. Then it's up to you to grow, care for and harvest it...and live the joys all over again when you use it in a special dish or drink from your kitchen.

Light Requirements

Full Sun. Prefers sun most of the day.

Light Shade. Prefers more shade than sun.

Full Shade. Prefers shade most or all of the time.

Usable Parts of Plant

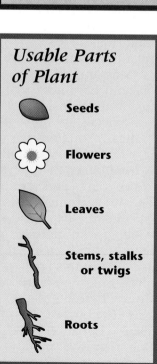

Seeds

Flowers

Leaves

Stems, stalks or twigs

Roots

Background and History

Harvest Strategies

Using in the Kitchen

Recipe Idea

Description

Growing and Caring Secrets

Non-Culinary Ideas

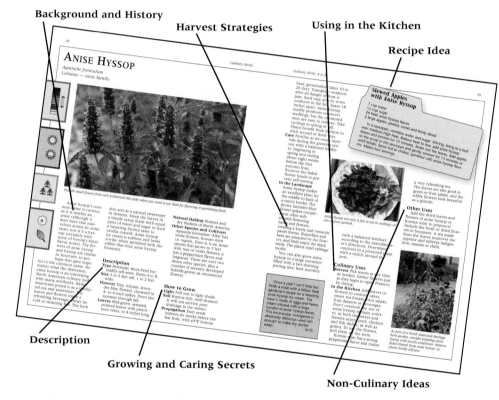

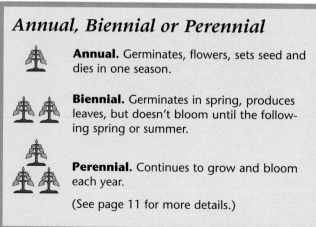

Annual, Biennial or Perennial

Annual. Germinates, flowers, sets seed and dies in one season.

Biennial. Germinates in spring, produces leaves, but doesn't bloom until the following spring or summer.

Perennial. Continues to grow and bloom each year.

(See page 11 for more details.)

Zone

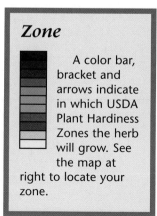

A color bar, bracket and arrows indicate in which USDA Plant Hardiness Zones the herb will grow. See the map at right to locate your zone.

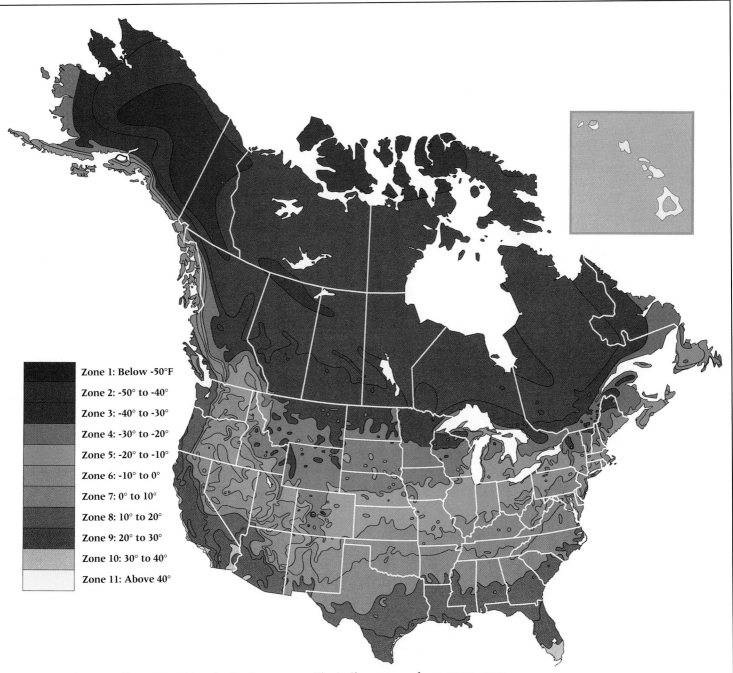

USDA Plant Hardiness Zone Map, indicating areas with similar average low temperatures.

Zone 1: Below -50°F
Zone 2: -50° to -40°
Zone 3: -40° to -30°
Zone 4: -30° to -20°
Zone 5: -20° to -10°
Zone 6: -10° to 0°
Zone 7: 0° to 10°
Zone 8: 10° to 20°
Zone 9: 20° to 30°
Zone 10: 30° to 40°
Zone 11: Above 40°

A NOTE ON OTHER USES

This book focuses on growing herbs successfully and then using them in the kitchen to help create beautiful, aromatic, wonderful-tasting foods.

Yet through the ages, some herbs have acquired special, almost medicinal status as natural cures for any one of a number of illnesses or ailments. Indigestion,

stress, colds, sore throats, stiff muscles...the list goes on. We make some of those suggestions here, based on what folklore and history tell us about each herb. Consider these ideas as suggestions only; the jury's still out, and in fact may never come in, on whether there's any merit to these non-culinary suggestions.

Bottom line? Seek professional medical help if you think you have a real medical problem. The herbal suggestions offered here are not cures; but who can argue that a warm cup of delightful herb tea, a hot bath steaming with herbal aromas or some other soothing herbal folk remedy won't make you feel just a little better?

ANGELICA

Angelica archangelica
Umbelliferae — carrot family

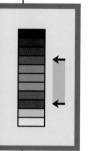

Angelica is great to use in the garden for its architectural form.

The stems of angelica are best harvested in early summer.

leaves and stems have the ability to bring sweetness to a dish, reducing the need for large amounts of sugar. You can also add leaves and stems to main course soups or stews. The roots are eaten as a vegetable. All parts flavor herb liqueurs.

Description

Type Biennial or short-lived perennial. Zones 4 to 9.
Size 4 to 8 feet tall, 3 feet wide.
Flowers Tiny, greenish-white flowers in globe-shaped clusters 4 to 8 inches across; honeylike fragrance. Late spring.
Leaves Dark green and celery-like, with oval, pointed, toothed leaflets to 3 inches long.
Natural Habitat Native to northern and eastern Europe, Greenland and central Asia.
Other Species and Cultivars *Angelica gigas* is an ornamental plant similar in appearance but with purple stems and flowers. Chinese angelica (*A.

The reasons for angelica's heavenly associations are lost in the mists of time, although in my region it does generally bloom around May 8, the feast day of St. Michael the Archangel. Once considered a great healing and magical herb, angelica is now prized for the drama it provides in the garden and the spicy sweet licorice taste it brings to foods. The British prefer to candy the stems for decorating pastry, but angelica's best use may be as an addition to rhubarb, gooseberry or other tart fruit desserts. The

Angelica and Rhubarb Pie

4 cups rhubarb stems, cut into ¹/₂
inch pieces
¹/₂ cup granulated sugar
¹/₃ cup unbleached all-purpose or
whole-wheat flour
¹/₄ cup fresh angelica stems,
and/or leaves, finely
chopped
One 9-inch unbaked pie crust
and top

Preheat oven to 400°F. In a
large bowl, combine rhubarb,
sugar, flour and angelica. Mix
thoroughly. Pour the rhubarb
mixture into the pie crust. Cover with the top
crust, crimping the edges and making several slits in it with a knife.
Bake for 15 minutes, then reduce heat to 350°F and cook for another 20
to 30 minutes or until the crust is golden brown. Makes one 9-inch pie.

Culinary Uses
Harvest Gather the leaves or stems in early summer before the plant flowers; the seeds when ripe in late summer and the roots in the autumn when they are one year old. Preserve by drying.

In the Kitchen Include fresh leaves in salads, sweet or savory soups, meat stews or fruit desserts. Add the seeds or roots to breads, cakes, cookies or other desserts. Flavor liqueurs with the seeds, stems or roots.

Other Uses
The dried seedheads make a dramatic addition to dried flower arrangements, while the leaves lend their spicy-sweet scent to potpourris. Or, burn the seed as incense. Drink a tea made from the leaves for stress, headaches, indigestion, coughs or colds, but do not use medicinally when pregnant. When you're tired or have sore muscles, add the leaves to your bathwater.

sinensis) is an important Chinese medicinal herb.

How to Grow
Light Light shade.
Soil Humus-rich, moist.
Propagation Sow fresh seed outdoors in early autumn.

Keep moist but do not cover, as seed requires light to germinate. Seed loses viability in three months, but it will keep up to a year if refrigerated in an airtight container. Thin to 3 feet apart. If seeds are not sown in place in the garden the previous autumn, transplant to the permanent site in mid-spring.

Care Remove flowers as they develop, to prolong the life of the plant. Let flowers develop on at least one plant to provide seed for new plants. Spray aphids or spider mites with horticultural soap.

In the Landscape Angelica makes a striking plant in the back of a moist, shady border. The flowers attract beneficial insects such as parasitic wasps.

Add the leaves of angelica to desserts, especially those made with tart fruits, to reduce the amount of sugar needed.

The leaves of angelica have been known to be cooled & eaten as a vegetable, too.

ANISE

Pimpinella anisum
Umbelliferae — carrot family

For many people, Christmas would not be the same without anise-flavored springerle cookies made in wooden molds. For others, anise is synonymous with liqueurs, such as pastis from France or ouzo from Greece. As after-dinner drinks, they aid digestion. The refined licorice flavor of anise plays a role in any number of other foods as well, from cuisines as diverse as Arabic, East Indian, Greek, Moroccan and Scandinavian. Cinnamon and bay complement anise seeds in pork or game dishes. Anise also has a long history of use for coughs and indigestion, with both Pythagoras and Hippocrates recommending it. In the sixteenth century, it was a popular bait for mousetraps.

Most often the seeds of anise are used in cooking, but the feathery leaves and white flowers are also edible and have a mild anise flavor.

The whole crushed seeds of anise have many uses from desserts to breads.

Description
Type Annual.
Size 2 feet tall, 1 to 2 feet wide.
Flowers Flat clusters of tiny, yellowish-white flowers. Summer.
Leaves Toothed, rounded to heart-shaped lower leaves. Feathery, deeply divided upper leaves.

Natural Habitat Native to Egypt and the Mediterranean.
Other Species and Cultivars Star anise is an unrelated evergreen tree native to China. The star-shaped fruits have a flavor similar to anise.

How to Grow
Light Full sun.
Soil Humus-rich, well-drained.
Propagation Because of its long taproot, anise is best started from seed sown directly into the garden when daytime temperatures are consistently 70°F or

Anise tends to be a floppy plant in the garden. Plant it among other herbs or flowers to help support it.

Besides its place in the vegetable garden, you can also grow anise as an ornamental in containers.

warmer. Thin to 1 foot apart.

Care Plants do tend to flop, so protect from strong winds with some type of support, such as twigs or commercially available plant supports. Or plant in groups of five so that they support each other.

In the Landscape Grow anise in rows or groups in the herb or vegetable garden. Anise enhances the growth of cilantro, repels aphids and cabbage moths and attracts beneficial parasitic wasps.

Anise also grows well in a deep container filled with a fast-draining potting mix and a monthly feeding with a balanced fertilizer according to the manufacturer's directions.

Culinary Uses

Add the whole, crushed or ground seeds to pastries, cakes, cookies, fruit desserts or breads. Also use them in pickles, curries, soups, stews, cooked greens or root vegetables. Anise also enhances egg or cheese dishes. Add fresh leaves or flowers to fruit or green salads or dips; make the dips with fresh cheese or sour cream.

Other Uses

Add the seed to potpourri. Dogs love anise just like cats enjoy catnip, so provide some, fresh or dried, for rolling around in. Chew the seeds after dinner to aid digestion and freshen breath. A tea made from the leaves or seeds is good for indigestion, coughs or colds. And don't forget to improve your complexion by adding ground seeds to face packs.

Figs in Anise Sherry

8 ounces dried figs
1 cup water
1/4 cup dry sherry
1 teaspoon anise seed, lightly crushed
2 tablespoons honey

In a bowl, combine figs, water, sherry and anise seed. Let soak for 2 hours. Put the fig mixture and the honey in a saucepan. Place over medium heat and bring to a boil, stirring occasionally. Reduce heat to low and cook for 20 minutes or until the figs are tender. Serve warm or at room temperature, with whipped cream or topping if desired. Makes four servings.

ANISE HYSSOP

Agastache foeniculum
Labiatae — mint family

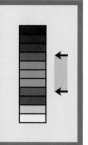

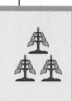

Pick the small flowers from each bottlebrush-like spike when you want to use them for flavoring or garnishing foods.

Anise hyssop's common name is curious, as it is neither an anise (although it does have that marvelous aromatic anise taste) nor is it a hyssop (certainly with none of hyssop's bitter flavor notes). The flowers of anise hyssop and hyssop are similar in structure, so perhaps that gave impetus to the common name. No matter what the derivation, anise hyssop is an interesting North American culinary herb with many attributes. Native Americans prized it as a medicinal tea and sweetener. The leaves and flowers make a refreshing beverage, either ice cold or steaming hot. The herb also acts as a natural sweetener in desserts. Steep the leaves in a simple syrup made with equal parts of water and sugar to lend a haunting licorice taste to vanilla custard. Anise hyssop ice cream is sublime and looks terrific when sprinkled with the edible lilac-blue anise hyssop blossoms.

Description
Type Perennial, short-lived but readily self-sows. Zones 4 to 8.
Size 3 to 5 feet tall, 1 to 2 feet wide.
Flowers Tiny, tubular, lavender-blue flowers, clustered in 4- to 6-inch spikes. From late summer through fall.
Leaves Mid-green, serrated, pointed leaves with prominent veins, to 4 inches long.

Natural Habitat Prairies and dry thickets of North America.
Other Species and Cultivars *Agastache foeniculum* 'Alba' has white flowers. Korean mint (*A. rugosa*), Zone 6, is an Asian species that grows to 5 feet with rose or violet flowers; it has a peppermint flavor and fragrance. There are over two dozen other species, plus a number of recently developed hybrids grown as ornamental flowers.

How to Grow
Light Full sun to light shade.
Soil Humus-rich, well-drained. It will not survive poor drainage in the winter.
Propagation Start seeds indoors six weeks before the last frost, with 65°F bottom

heat; germination takes 10 to 20 days. Transplant outdoors after all danger of frost is past. Seed may also be sown outdoors in the fall. Space 18 inches apart. Anise hyssop readily produces volunteer seedlings, but the unwanted ones are easy to remove. Take cuttings in spring or fall. Plants benefit from division in their second or third year.

Care Fertilize at six-week intervals during the growing season with a balanced fertilizer, beginning in spring and ending about eight weeks before the first autumn frost. Remove the faded flower heads to prevent self-sowing.

In the Landscape

Anise hyssop makes an excellent plant for the middle to back of a sunny border. The showy lavender-blue flower spikes complement other soft-colored flowering herbs and flowers, creating a lovely and romantic pastel theme. Butterflies and bees are attracted by the flowers, and birds enjoy the black seeds. The plants repel cabbage moths.

You can also grow anise hyssop in a large container filled with a fast-draining potting mix; feed monthly with a

> Once a year I can't help but finish a meal with a fellow herb gardener's recipe for a heavenly anise hyssop ice cream. The base is made of eggs and heavy cream infused with a large handful of anise hyssop leaves. This once-a-year indulgence is absolutely delicious—and rich enough to make my doctor weep.   M.O.

Stewed Apples with Anise Hyssop

1 cup water
1/2 cup sugar
24 fresh anise hyssop leaves
2 large apples: peeled, cored and thinly sliced

In a saucepan, combine water and sugar. Stirring, bring to a boil over medium-high heat. Reduce heat to low, add anise hyssop leaves and simmer for 15 minutes. Strain out the leaves. Add apples to the syrup in the saucepan and gently simmer for 15 minutes or until tender. Serve hot or chilled, sprinkled with anise hyssop flowers. Makes four servings.

Anise Hyssop is fun to use in cooking—and also makes a great garnish.

balanced fertilizer according to the manufacturer's directions. Overwinter outdoors in a protected place with a mulch around the pots.

Culinary Uses

Harvest Pick leaves at any time as needed. Gather flowers just as they begin to open. Preserve by drying.

In the Kitchen Add leaves or flowers to cookies, cakes, sweet tea breads, fruit salads, fruit desserts or beverages. Don't overlook the use of anise hyssop in main courses, as both the leaves and flowers accent pork, chicken and fish dishes, as well as grains. To use the flowers, pull them off the stem.

Korean mint has a strong peppermint flavor and makes a very refreshing tea. The leaves are also good in green or fruit salads, and the edible flowers look beautiful as a garnish.

Other Uses

Add the dried leaves and flowers of anise hyssop or Korean mint to potpourri. Include the fresh or dried flowers in bouquets. A tea made from the leaves improves the appetite and relieves indigestion, nausea or chills.

As part of a North American heritage herb garden, consider planting anise hyssop with purple coneflower. Remove faded blooms from anise hyssop, as the plants boldly self-sow.

BASIL

Ocimum basilicum
Labiatae — mint family

Many people consider basil the quintessential summer herb, using it minced and sprinkled over tomatoes or made into pesto sauce.

Basil is known as the king of herbs, as its name derives from the Greek word meaning royal. Taste-wise it is most deserving of the title with its blend of clove, mint and mild pepper. There are upwards of 150 species of annual basils that are native to the warmer regions of Africa, Asia and Central and South America, plus dozens more cultivars. Of these, the following are among the best choices for delivering flavor in the kitchen and beauty to the garden.

'Genovese' basil is said to be "the perfume of Genoa and the soul of pesto." Using basil for pesto is ancient, for historians have traced its use to the time of the early Roman poet Virgil. He described a paste of herbs, garlic, olive oil and cheese smeared on bread for breakfast. If pesto is your passion, 'Genovese' and 'Piccolo Verde Fino' are the ones for you. It is a toss up as to which one makes the most flavorful pesto.

'Genovese', the similar 'Genoa Green Improved' and 'Genoa Profumastissima' grow to 2 feet high, with long, pointed, glossy leaves to 3 inches long with an intensely per-fumed scent and flavor. They are exceptionally vigorous growers, producing lush foliage on many-branched plants. Gardeners can harvest the herb in abundance all summer long. 'Piccolo Verde Fino' also grows to 2 feet tall, but has leaves only 1 inch long.

The "lettuce-leaf" basils are another group with traditional flavor and scent. They have extra-large, crinkled or smooth leaves to 6 inches long on 2-foot plants. Varieties include 'Mammoth', 'Napoletano' and 'Valentino'. 'Green Ruffles' has exceptionally puckered leaves.

'Mrs. Burns' Lemon', as its name implies, has a wonderully pungent citrus note in its light green, 2-inch leaves on 3-foot plants. Many gardeners feel it has a richer lemon prescence than lemon basil (*O. ctiriodorum*). Don't fail to try another lemon basil, 'Sweet Dani', an All-America Selection winner.

Basil is a great container herb and can be very ornamental as well.

A chef from Genoa once shared his pesto secret with me. Add some sweet marjoram (see page 140) along with the basil, garlic, olive oil, cheese and pine nuts. Or, add a handful of parsley. He also told me to mix pesto with green beans and potatoes as well as with pasta.

'Aussie Sweetie' is an unusual basil in that it doesn't require constantly pinching out of the flower heads. In fact, it hardly ever flowers. Growing as a narrow column to 2 feet, it has 2-inch leaves with a sweet and subtle blend of mint and cloves. 'Greek Columnar' basil is similar.

With the popularity of Southeast Asian cuisine, 'Siam Queen' combines the best of appearance and the characteristic anise-licorice-lemon-cinnamon flavors of the basils from the Pacific Rim. Growing to 2 feet tall, 'Siam Queen' has a dramatic appearance, with turrets of young, deep crimson leaves above the older, rich green leaves.

Among the basils with other flavors, look for 'Anise', 'Licorice', 'Spice', 'Mexican Spice' and 'Cinnamon'.

'Red Rubin' is a highly ornamental, 2-foot basil, effective as a punctuation in the garden. It maintains a purplish color throughout the summer. It is a selection from 'Dark Opal' basil, which tends to lose the intense color as the season goes along. Other purple-leaved basils include 'Purple Ruffles' and 'Osmin'.

Although they can be used in cooking, the dwarf basils are mainly prized for their diminutive form in pots or as edgings. With a rounded shape, they grow to 1 foot tall with 1-inch leaves. Varieties include 'Bush Green', 'Dwarf Bouquet', 'Dwarf Bush', 'Dwarf Bush Fine Leaf', 'Dwarf Italian', 'Green Bouquet', 'Green Globe', 'Miniature', 'Spicy Bush' and 'Spicy Globe'.

'Siam Queen' is a hybrid form of the Thai basil, with its anise-licorice-lemon-cinnamon flavor.

The various forms of purple basils, with their deeply-colored leaves, complement flowers in the garden. Here, they're paired with golden coreopsis.

Try using 'Licorice' basil in desserts, especially those with fruits such as peaches, apricots and nectarines.

Description
Type Tender annual.
Size 1 to 3 feet tall, 1 to 2 feet wide.
Flowers Spikes of $^1/_2$-inch white flowers in summer.
Leaves Bright green, oval, pointed, 1 to 6 inches long.
Natural Habitat Native to India, Africa and Asia.
Other Species and Cultivars Camphor basil (*O. kilimand-scharicum*) grows to 3 feet tall and has a camphor scent. 'African Blue', a hybrid with this and 'Dark Opal', has purplish leaves fading to green. East Indian basil (*O. gratissimum*) grows to 6 feet tall with 7-inch, pungently scented leaves useful for repelling insects. Holy, or tulsi basil (*O. tenuiflorum*, syn. *O. sanctum*), sacred to Hindus, has medicinal uses, while 'Sacred' is a citrus-and-spice culinary herb.

'Spicy Globe' basil grows naturally into a smooth, round ball shape, making it an unusal accent in the garden or an easy-to-grow edging.

How to Grow
Light Full sun.
Soil Humus-rich, moist, well-drained.
Propagation Start seed indoors four weeks before the last frost, planting $^1/_8$ inch deep and with 75°F bottom heat; germination takes about 3 days. Set out when all danger of frost is past and night temperatures are above 65°F. Seed can also be sown direct-ly into the garden at this time. Space plants 12 to 18 inches apart.
Care Fertilize at six-week inter-vals during the growing sea-son with a balanced organic fertilizer. Remove the flower spikes as they emerge to keep the plant bushy and produc-ing new leaves.
In the Landscape Basils read-ily fit in ornamental borders or beds as well as an herb or vegetable garden. Basils are a great companion plant for peppers and tomatoes, plus they repel aphids, mites and tomato hornworms. The purple-leaved forms plus 'African Blue' and 'Siam Queen' are especially good for creating stunning effects, whether with pink and pas-tel flowers or in bolder

Eggplant and Basil Spread

1 eggplant (about 1 pound)
1/2 cup finely chopped sweet onion, such as Vidalia
1/2 cup peeled, seeded and finely chopped fresh tomatoes
1/2 cup seeded and finely chopped roasted red peppers
1/4 cup finely chopped fresh basil
1/4 cup finely chopped fresh parsley
1 garlic clove, minced
2 tablespoons white wine vinegar
2 tablespoons extra-virgin olive oil
1/2 teaspoon salt
1/8 teaspoon ground black pepper

Place whole eggplant in a large saucepan with water to cover. Bring to a boil over high heat, reduce heat to low, then simmer until the eggplant is easily pierced with a fork. Drain, cool, peel and mash the eggplant. In a bowl, combine the eggplant with the onion, tomato, red pepper, basil, parsley, garlic, vinegar, olive oil, salt and pepper. Stir until well blended. Store in an airtight container overnight to allow flavors to blend. Serve as a dip or sandwich filling. Makes about 2 cups.

late summer for wintering inside.

Culinary Uses

Harvest Pick leaves at any time. Gather flowers as they open. The flavor of the leaves is best preserved by freezing, but even dried basil is better than none at all.

In the Kitchen The basils are traditional in Italian, Mediterranean and Thai cooking. Try them with almost any vegetable, as well as with lamb, fish, poultry, soups, stews, cheese or eggs. They blend particularly well with garlic, thyme, parsley and lemon. Or, make wonderfully flavored vinegars. Lemon, Thai and cinnamon basils are also good in cookies and fruit desserts.

combinations dominated by orange and yellow. Or, try a monochromatic effect with bronze fennel. The dwarf forms are superb as edgings for beds.

The basils easily adapt to containers filled with a fast-draining potting mix. Feed monthly with a balanced fertilizer according to the manufacturer's directions. Bring pots indoors during the winter or start new plants in

Other Uses

Use stems in fresh bouquets, especially for outdoor eating, as basil repels many flying insects. Dried basil leaves and flowers add a sweet fragrance to potpourris. Make a tea from the leaves for headaches, indigestion, colds or stress. Splash basil infusion on your body to repel mosquitoes. The leaves make an invigorating addition to bathwater and a basil rinse makes hair shine.

The quilted, ruffly leaves of 'Green Ruffles' basil lend it to use as an ornamental among flowers.

It's hard to pick just one basil to grow. Some of the choices include 'Purple Ruffles', 'Siam Queen', 'Genovese', 'Licorice', 'Spicy Globe' and 'Finissimo a Palla'.

BAY

Laurus nobilis
Lauraceae — laurel family

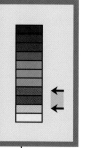

Declared eternally sacred by Apollo, Greek god of the sun, bay leaves woven into garlands have crowned the heads of kings and poets as well as the victors of battle, athletic competitions and scholarly contests. Because it was a symbol of honor and greatness, bay was also thought to protect against and relieve any number of ills. Today, a bay wreath is more likely to grace a kitchen wall, and the leaves are valued for their aromatic virtues in stocks, soups, stews or marinades. Bay combines particularly well with black pepper, garlic, allspice, mustard, saffron and lemon. For many people, it may come as a surprise that you can give baked custard and vanilla pudding a wonderful flavor by steeping bay leaves in the milk before preparing them.

Description

Type Woody, evergreen shrub or tree. Zones 8 to 10.
Size Up to 50 feet when grown year-round outdoors; 5 to 10 feet in containers.
Flowers Inconspicuous, greenish-yellow flowers. Spring.
Leaves Dark green, leathery, oval, pointed leaves, to 3 inches long.
Natural Habitat Mediterranean and Asia Minor.

Other Species and Cultivars

'Angustifolia' has leaves with wavy edges. 'Aurea' has leaves tinged with yellow.

How to Grow

Light Full sun to light shade.
Soil Humus-rich, well-drained.

Propagation Difficult to start from seed, but if you're feeling adventurous, try them indoors with 75°F bottom heat; germination takes four weeks. Cuttings are much more reliable, but still a slow process. Take cuttings in the fall from young shoots; root-

Bay is a wonderful plant, though most gardeners have to grow this tree in containers so it can be indoors during winter.

Bay naturally grows upward into a tree form, but if you continually pinch out the growing tips, the plant becomes bushy.

Lentil Salad

$^1/_2$ cup French lentils (or substitute brown lentils)
1 bay leaf
1 cup finely chopped onion
$^1/_2$ teaspoon salt
$^1/_4$ teaspoon freshly ground black pepper
1 cup peeled, seeded and chopped tomatoes
2 tablespoons minced, fresh parsley
2 tablespoons extra-virgin olive oil
2 tablespoons lemon juice
$^1/_2$ teaspoon Dijon mustard

In a large saucepan, combine lentils, bay leaf, onion, salt and pepper. Cover with cold water. Bring to a boil over high heat. Reduce heat to low, cover, then simmer for 40 minutes or until lentils are tender, adding water if necessary. Drain and remove bay leaf. Stir in tomatoes and parsley. In a small bowl, whisk the olive oil, lemon juice and mustard together. Pour over the lentil mixture and combine thoroughly. Serve at room temperature or chilled. Makes four servings.

ing may take six to nine months.

Care Except where hardy, grow bay in containers filled with a fast-draining potting mix and overwinter indoors. Fertilize in the spring with a balanced fertilizer according to the manufacturer's directions. Pinch out tip growth to encourage branching. Bay is very susceptible to scale. Control with sprays of horticultural soap or a summer horticultural oil.

In the Landscape A well-grown potted bay tree makes a stunning focal point in the garden in summer. As a movable object, potted bays may grace a patio one day then the front entrance or a buffet table the next. Bay also adapts well to being grown as a standard topiary.

Culinary Uses

Harvest Pick bay leaves for use at any time, choosing the older leaves. Because bay leaves curl as they dry, some gardeners dry them in a flower press or between sheets of newsprint with a heavy object on top. The leaves are usually dry in about two weeks.

In the Kitchen Add a bay leaf to soup stock, soups, stews, marinades, roasts, tomato sauce, pickles or shellfish boils. Just remember to remove the bay leaf before serving. Steep a bay leaf in scalded milk before making pudding or custard. Use leaves in flavoring herbal vinegars, too.

Other Uses

Make an entire wreath of bay leaves or include several leaves along with other herbs in wreaths or crafts. Place bay leaves in containers of flour, rice, grains or dried figs to help deter weevils. Drink a tea made from bay leaves for indigestion or pour on your hair as a rinse to treat dandruff. Add bay leaves to bathwater to relieve joint or muscle pain.

The glossy, leathery leaves of bay lend a rich undertone to stews, soups and roasts. For an interesting change, try steeping the leaves in milk before making custard.

BERGAMOT

Monard didyma
Labiatae — mint family

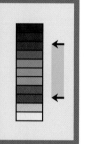

Encourage second bloom by cutting bergamot back to the ground after the first flowering. This also limits problems from mildew.

Description

Type Perennial. Zones 3 to 9.

Size 1 to 3 feet tall, 1 to 2 feet wide.

Flowers Clusters of scarlet tubular florets to 2 inches long.

Leaves Dark green, oval, pointed, with toothed edges and slightly rough surface, to 3 inches long.

Natural Habitat Native to eastern and southern North America.

Other Species and Cultivars

Dozens of cultivars have been developed, mainly differing in flower color and resistance to powdery mildew. The color range includes scarlet, burgundy, mauve, pink, violet, lavender and white. Some of the most disease-resistant cultivars include 'Marshall's Delight', growing to 3 feet tall with rich pink flowers, 'Gardenview Scarlet', growing to 30 inches with red flowers and 'Sioux', growing to 4 feet tall with pinkish-white flowers.

Gardeners may first think of bergamot, also known as bee balm, as a stalwart of summer-blooming perennial gardens. This North American native is no less notable for the colorful addition the edible flowers bring to food and drink, plus the delightful citrus-mint tang of the leaves. It is the scent, reminiscent of bergamot oranges, that provides the common name. Early settlers found Native Americans utilizing bergamot both for a pleasant drink and as a medicine for coughs and sore throats. Historical folklore has bergamot used as a replacement for black tea by the colonists after the Boston Tea Party.

The flowers of bergamot can range from red to pink to bluish purple to white—a color for every dish!

A number of hybrid cultivars of the American native bergamot exist, with colors including mauve, burgundy, pink and white.

New for the garden are dwarf monarda cultivars 'Petite Delight' and 'Petite Wonder'. Both have lavender pink flowers on 1-foot plants with mildew resistance.

For the wild garden, there is wild monarda (*M. fistulosa*), Zone 3, with lavender flowers on 3-foot plants, and horsemint (*M. punctata*), Zone 5, with purple-spotted, yellow, 1-inch flowers in tiers of dense whorls on 2-foot plants; both are perennials tolerant of dry soil. Lemon mint (*M. citriodora*) is an annual noteworthy for its lemon-scented leaves and pinkish-purple flowers.

How to Grow

Light Full sun to light shade.

Soil Humus-rich, moist, well-drained.

Propagation Although bergamot can be propagated from seeds, germinating in two weeks, the plants are highly variable and take at least two years to reach maturity. To have plants that are the same as the parent, propagate bergamot by division in spring or autumn. Space plants 2 feet apart.

Care Choose a site that gets good air circulation, as this helps to prevent powdery mildew. Another deterrent is to cut the plants back to the ground after flowering. This also often causes plants to bloom again in the autumn.

In the Landscape We can be justly proud of this native plant, as it is exceptionally handsome in ornamental flower borders. So just think what it can do for the herb garden. Hummingbirds are a constant visitor to the red-flowered forms, while bumble bees and butterflies delight in any color.

Culinary Uses

Harvest Pick the leaves anytime you need them. Gather the flowers just as they

The edible flowers of bergamot are a natural for garnishing a platter of appetizers for a party. They also look pretty in drinks.

become fully open. Preserve both by drying.

In the Kitchen Both the fresh flowers or leaves are a delight in either tossed green salads or with fresh fruit. Use fresh or dried leaves or flowers in cooked fruit desserts, and in recipes with duck, pork or sausages. Bergamot also adds a lovely note to jellies and jams. Blend it with black tea, lemonade or white wines.

Other Uses

Dried flowers and leaves add color and fragrance to potpourris. A tea made from the leaves eases colds, indigestion, insomnia or menstrual cramps. This infusion is also a fragrant addition to bath water.

The nectar-rich florets on each bergamot flower head attract hummingbirds and butterflies. People like them too, in fruit salads or desserts.

Blueberry-Melon Compote with Lemon-Bergamot Sauce

8 ounces lemon yogurt
1/4 cup minced, fresh bergamot leaves
1 cup fresh blueberries
1 1/2 cups fresh cantaloupe, cut into 1-inch cubes
Fresh bergamot petals

In a small bowl, combine yogurt and bergamot leaves. Cover and refrigerate for at least an hour. In another bowl, combine blueberries and cantaloupe, then spoon into serving dishes. Pour the yogurt mixture over the fruit. Garnish with bergamot petals and serve. Makes four servings.

BORAGE

Borago officinalis
Boraginaceae — borage family

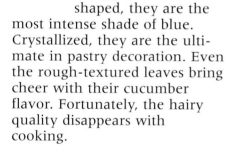

If only the Cowardly Lion had known of borage, perhaps he could have saved himself the trouble of venturing down that yellow brick road. Soldiers going into battle in ancient times partook of wine steeped with borage to shore up their nerve. Nero's physician, Dioscorides, wrote that borage could "cheer the heart and lift the depressed spirits." Sad to say, it may have been the wine rather than the borage, as modern research gives no credence to these uses. Without question though, the edible flowers of borage do bring pleasure. Star-shaped, they are the most intense shade of blue. Crystallized, they are the ultimate in pastry decoration. Even the rough-textured leaves bring cheer with their cucumber flavor. Fortunately, the hairy quality disappears with cooking.

Description

Type Annual.
Size 2 feet tall, 2 feet wide.
Flowers Drooping clusters of 1-inch, blue, star-shaped flowers with a white-and-black center.
Leaves Oval, deeply veined, bristly, gray-green leaves to 6 inches long.
Natural Habitat Native to Europe, Asia Minor, northern Europe and Africa.

Other Species and Cultivars
Borago officinalis 'Alba' has white flowers.

How to Grow

Light Full sun to light shade.

Soil Humus-rich, moist, well-drained.
Propagation Sow the seed directly into the garden after all danger of frost has passed. Space plants to 2 feet apart. Borage does not

In addition to the beauty of the flowers, the mild cucumber flavor of borage leaves plays a role in salads, herb cheeses and cooked greens.

Borage's beautiful, star-shaped, blue flowers more than make up for the plant's sprawling nature.

Borage Tea Sandwiches

4 large eggs, hard-boiled, peeled and diced
1/4 cup mayonnaise
2 tablespoons minced fresh borage leaves
1/2 teaspoon Dijon mustard
1/4 teaspoon salt
8 slices of thin-sliced bread
Butter

In a bowl, combine the mayonnaise, borage, mustard and salt. Combine thoroughly. Trim the crusts from the bread and thinly spread with butter. Divide the egg mixture between four slices of buttered bread. Top with the remaining bread. Cut into three pieces. Makes 12 sandwiches. As an alternative, leave the sandwiches open-faced and garnish with fresh borage blossoms.

transplant well, but if necessary, do so when the plants are very young, disturbing the roots as little as possible.

Care Borage grows best in the cool weather of spring and autumn. Keep the blooms picked so that the plant continues to flower. Allow a few blooms to go to seed as these will self-sow. Spray aphids with horticultural soap.

In the Landscape Borage is not a plant for formal gardens as it tends to sprawl. Make the most of this tendency by placing plants at the edges of raised beds or at the tops of low walls. The foliage blends well with silver- or gray-leaved plants. Borage is thought to strengthen plants growing near it.

Borage grows well in a container filled with a fast-draining potting mix. Feed monthly with a balanced fertilizer according to the manufacturer's directions.

Culinary Uses

Harvest Gather young leaves as you need them for fresh use. There is no way to preserve them except by capturing the flavor in vinegar. Pick flowers just as they open, preserving them by drying.

In the Kitchen The flowers make an appealing garnish in punches, iced drinks, salads or fresh fruit dishes, although acid foods do turn them pink. Freeze flowers in ice cubes or crystallize with sugar. Mince the leaves and include them in salads, soups, cooked greens, butters, dips or sandwiches. Use with dishes that feature eggs, cheese, fish or poultry. They're also traditional in Pimm's or white wine. Because of the high mineral content, the leaves are a beneficial addition to herb-seasoning blends. Flavor vinegar with either the leaves or flowers.

Other Uses

Add a charming touch to bouquets with stems of the fresh flowers. Include the dried flowers in potpourri for their color. Drink a tea made from the leaves for colds, coughs, insomnia or stress.

Borage flowers are among the most flavorful of edible flowers. Create elaborate decoration on foods, such as this cheesecake.

It's not uncommon to see bumblebees visiting borage blooms.

CALENDULA

Calendula officinalis
Compositae — daisy family

Calendulas are usually thought of as golden, but orange and apricot flowers also come in some seed mixes.

Calendula is a cheerful, old-fashioned annual flower that was once such a popular herb that the dried petals were sold by the barrel. The Elizabethan herbalist John Gerard wrote that no serious soup was without it. Calendula's bittersweet flavor brings an intriguing note both to main courses and desserts. The ability of the petals to impart their color to foods gave rise to the common name "poor man's saffron."

Calendulas are the marigolds of Shakespeare writings and John Keats' poems. Other monikers include marybud, bulls eye, holligold, poor man's saffron and pot marigold, which most specifically refers to it's use in the cooking pot. With the flowers turning their faces to the sun as the day progresses, it has also been called the "herb of the sun" or the "husbandman's dial." The genus name is derived from the Latin *calends*, or the first day of every month, as the plants were in bloom year-round in ancient Rome.

Description

Type Annual. Withstands temperatures to 30°F.

Size 8 to 24 inches tall, 1 foot wide.

Flowers Yellow to orange, 2 to 4 inch daisy-like flowers. Spring through fall; flowers best in cooler weather.

Leaves Soft-textured, light green, narrow, oval leaves to 3 inches long.

Natural Habitat Native to southern and central Europe and northern Africa.

Other Species and Cultivars For herbal uses, it's easiest to harvest large petals, such as those from 'Pacific Beauty', a variety that grows to 18 inches tall with flowers of mixed colors.

How to Grow

Light Full sun but tolerates light shade in hot climates.

Soil Humus-rich, well-drained.

Propagation Start seed indoors six weeks before the last frost, with 65°F bottom heat; germination takes about a week. Sow seed directly into the garden when the soil temperature is 60°F, or about two weeks before the last frost. Thin to 10 inches apart. In Zones 9 and 10, seed may also be sown outdoors in late fall. Plants sometimes self-sow, if seeds are allowed to develop on plants.

Care Remove faded flowers to prolong blooming. Control slugs with bait or barriers. Spray aphids or whiteflies with horticultural soap. Pick off leaves with mildew and destroy them.

In the Landscape With their bright, sunny flowers, calendulas brighten flower beds as well as herb or vegetable gar-

The yellow or orange flowers of calendula contrast nicely in the herb garden with blue flowers, such as borage.

Calendula flowers work great in desserts, such as these lemon bars.

In growing calendulas for cooking, choose varieties that have large, wide petals, such as 'Pacific Beauty'.

In the Kitchen

Toss in some leaves with a mixed green salad or add them to a mixture of cooked greens. Fresh petals can also be added to salads. Fresh or dry, the petals flavor and color soups, stews, egg dishes, sandwich fillings, cheese dips and spreads, butters, grains or rice. Or, try petals in cakes, cookies or puddings, either adding them directly or steeping in the liquid used in the dessert. They also add a unique note to vinegars, liqueurs or white wines. Try them with yellow tomato or yellow plum jam.

Other Uses

Calendulas last as long as cut flowers. They also dry easily, adding color to potpourri or crafts. Drink a tea of calendula petals for indigestion or menstrual cramps. That same tea also makes a beneficial facial tonic, hair rinse for shiny highlights or a soothing and softening addition to bathwater.

dens. Obviously, the flowers blend well with other hot colored flowers such as tithonia, sunflowers, nasturtiums and the *Tagetes* marigolds. But experiment with plantings that combine them with purple and blue flowers.

Calendulas readily grow in containers filled with a fast-draining potting mix. Feed monthly with a balanced fertilizer according to the manufacturer's directions.

Culinary Uses

Harvest Young leaves are the most tender and tasty. Pick the flowers just as they open, pulling the petals from the flower heads. Preserve these by drying.

Calendula Muffins

1/2 cup (1 stick or 4 ounces) butter
1/2 cup sugar
2 large eggs
2 cups unbleached all-purpose flour
2 teaspoons baking powder
1/4 teaspoon salt
1/2 cup milk
1/2 cup fresh calendula petals

Preheat oven to 350°F. Spray muffin pans with non-stick cooking spray or line with paper muffin cups. In a large bowl, cream butter and sugar. Add eggs and beat well. Sift together flour, baking powder and salt. Alternately add flour mixture and milk, beating well after each addition. Stir in the calendula petals, combining thoroughly. Pour into muffin pans, filling each cup one-half full. Bake for 20 minutes or until golden brown. Makes a dozen muffins.

Calendula, an easily grown annual, brings bright, zingy color to gardens. The flowers are unusual in that they open and close with the sun.

CARAWAY

Carum carvi
Umbelliferae — carrot family

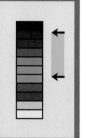

Caraway's clusters of edible white flowers eventually yield the brown seeds that are a favorite for flavoring cabbage dishes and rye bread.

Some people could not imagine rye bread or cabbage without caraway seeds. But that is just the tip of the culinary iceberg, for caraway plays a role in everything from appetizers to desserts to potent liqueurs such as aquavit from Scandinavia. With a flavor that has been compared to a combination of anise and dill, caraway seeds are used whole or ground. What many people don't realize is that the fresh leaves bring a lighter touch to foods, while you can dig the roots in autumn and cook them as a vegetable. Although often associated with Nordic countries or Germany, caraway's history extends back to the ancient Egyptians, who included it in the tombs of the Pharoahs. Remnants of seed have even been found in Stone Age dwelling sites.

Description

Type Biennial, often grown as an annual. Zones 3 to 9.
Size 2 feet tall, 2 feet wide.

Caraway seeds have been used in just about all kinds of dishes around the world.

Flowers Flat heads of tiny white flowers, to 4 inches across. Summer.

Leaves Feathery, finely cut leaves to 10 inches long. Leaves stay green during winter in Zone 8 or warmer.

Natural Habitat Native to Asia, the Middle East and central Europe.

How to Grow

Light Full sun.

Soil Humus-rich, moist, well-drained.

Propagation Sow seed directly into the garden, 1/2 inch deep, two weeks before the last frost in spring or in early autumn. You'll get the best germination with fresh seed sown in autumn. Thin to 1 foot apart. Because of the taproot, caraway does not transplant well.

Care A summer mulch to maintain even soil moisture is especially important with caraway. Protect plants in winter with a loose mulch of pine boughs.

In the Landscape Caraway is a fine-textured addition to the herb or vegetable garden.

Caraway adapts to containers filled with a fast-draining potting mix and a monthly feeding with a balanced fertilizer according to manufacturer's directions.

Culinary Uses

Harvest Gather young leaves as you need them. Flavor is lost with all preserving methods. Timing is everything with the 1/4-inch ridged, crescent-shaped seeds. Wait until they're brown, but before they begin to fall, clip the stems and dry the seeds. Dig up the roots in autumn after the seeds are harvested.

In the Kitchen Caraway seeds become bitter with long cooking, so add to soups or stews 15 minutes before serving. Consider caraway seeds with eggs, cheese dishes, creamed soups or sauces, pork, beef or goose. The seeds also enhance most vegetables as well as apples, pickles, breads, cookies or cakes. Candy the seeds for a healthy nibble after dinner. Garnish soup with the leaves or try them with eggs, salads, vinegars, butters or dips.

Coleslaw with Caraway Dressing

2 1/2 cups shredded cabbage
1/2 cup shredded carrot
1/2 cup sweet green pepper, finely diced
1/2 cup sweet red pepper, finely diced
1 cup finely diced celery
1/4 cup fresh chives, minced
1/4 cup canola oil
2 tablespoons orange juice
2 tablespoons lemon juice
2 teaspoons caraway seeds, lightly crushed
1/2 teaspoon salt
1/4 teaspoon ground black pepper

In a large bowl, combine cabbage, carrot, green and red peppers, celery and chives. In a small bowl, whisk together oil, orange and lemon juices, caraway seeds, salt and pepper. Pour over the cabbage mixture and toss thoroughly. Cover and chill before serving. Makes six servings.

Other Uses

Nibble caraway seeds after dinner to sweeten breath and enhance digestion. A tea made from the seeds serves the same purpose.

When in bloom, caraway resembles its close relatives Queen Anne's lace and carrots. Planted in a mass, it enriches any garden.

CHERVIL

Anthriscus cerefolium
Umbelliferae — carrot family

Chervil is a decorative, lacy-leaved herb with a delicate taste of anise and parsley. Along with chives, parsley and tarragon, chervil makes up the classic French combination called *fines herbes*. Chervil flourishes in the cool months of the gardening season, making chervil soup a traditional accompaniment to Easter celebrations. The flavor is subtle and warming. As you begin to use it, you'll find more and more uses for chervil in your cooking. For further encouragement, consider that it is rich in vitamin C, carotene, iron and magnesium. Add it near the end of preparing food; long cooking turns chervil bitter.

Chervil's delicate flavor combines those of anise and parsley. Once you start using chervil, you'll find more and more foods to try it with.

Description
Type Annual.

With its ferny appearance, chervil is attractive in the garden, and complements many flowers such as this annual poppy.

Size 12 to 18 inches tall, 12 inches wide.
Flowers Flat clusters of tiny white flowers.
Leaves Fernlike leaves to 10 inches long.
Natural Habitat Native to Europe and Asia.
Other Species and Cultivars 'Crispum' has finely curled leaves.

How to Grow
Light Light shade.
Soil Humus-rich, moist, well-drained.
Propagation Chervil does not readily transplant, so it is best to sow the seed directly into the garden about four weeks before the last frost. Make a furrow 1 inch deep and sprinkle in the seed but do not cover. Mist the area lightly each day. Germination takes about 10 days and is best with fresh seed. Thin to 6 inches apart.
Care Chervil tends to bloom quickly. To ensure a continued harvest, sow seed every

Avocado with Chervil

2 avocados
2 tablespoons lemon juice
4 tablespoons low-fat or non-fat sour cream
2 tablespoons fresh chervil, finely minced
1/2 teaspoon salt
1/4 teaspoon ground black pepper

Cut the avocados in half and remove the pits. Scoop out the flesh, being careful not to damage the skin. In a small bowl, combine the avocado with the lemon juice. Add the sour cream, chervil, salt and pepper. Place the mixture back in the avocado shells. Cover with plastic wrap and chill in the refrigerator. Garnish with extra minced chervil and serve with slices of French bread. Makes four servings.

You can also plant chervil seeds directly into a deep container.

Chervil flowers work great with vegetable dishes.

two weeks until June. Begin sowing seeds again in late summer for an autumn crop. Chervil readily overwinters in a coldframe. Allow chervil to self-sow.

In the Landscape With its feathery foliage, chervil provides a soft texture in shaded gardens, perhaps planted beneath shrubs. Why not have it be part of a spring border, combining it with pansies, daffodils, tulips and Iceland poppies? Or, it could be part of a mesclun planting in the kitchen garden.

Chervil makes an excellent container plant, perhaps planted with edible flowers such as violas, Johnny-jump-ups and calendulas. Chervil is also a good choice for growing indoors. Use a fast-draining potting mix, and feed monthly with a balanced fertilizer according to the manufacturer's directions.

Culinary Uses

Harvest Leaves are ready to harvest six to eight weeks after sowing the seed. Pick from the outside rather than the center. Preserve by freezing.

In the Kitchen Include chervil leaves in salads, vegetables, fish, chicken or eggs. Add chervil to creamed hot or cold soups, and sauces. Vinegars and butters are both good ways to preserve chervil's flavor.

 TIP Soften the bitter taste of braised endive with a sprinkling of chervil just before serving. Chervil is my favorite culinary companion to peas, asparagus and artichokes.

Other Uses

When chervil starts to bloom, cut the flowers to include in bouquets. Both the dried leaves and flowers may be added to potpourri. Drink a tea made from the leaves for indigestion or use it as a facial tonic.

An annual, chervil should be planted directly into the garden rather than transplanted. Growing best in cool weather, plant chervil whenever you sow lettuce seed.

CHIVES

Allium schoenoprasum
Liliaceae — lily family

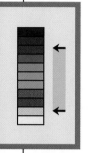

Because chives are such a familiar faithful in the herb garden, we sometimes overlook the wonderful attributes they bring to food. With their sweet, delicate onion flavor, chives add a wonderful accent when used as a garnish or added in the last few minutes of cooking. They combine especially well with dishes containing shallots, marjoram or tarragon. For some fun with your food, use a single chive to tie up small bundles of julienned carrots, haricot verts or pencil-thin asparagus stalks. Chives are prolific and provide their thin tubular stems from early spring to late fall. An added bonus: the bright fuchsia-pink flowers in spring, which make a lovely garnish in their own right. The flowers also make a beautifully colored vinegar.

Description
Type Perennial. Zones 3 to 10.
Size 12 to 18 inches tall, 12 to 18 inches wide.
Flowers Globe-shaped, 1-inch clusters of small lavender-pink flowers. Early summer.
Leaves Hollow, dark green leaves about $1/8$-inch thick.
Natural Habitat Native to Europe.
Other Species and Cultivars 'Forescate' grows to 24 inch-

es tall and the flowers are more distinctly pink. 'Profusion' is a long-blooming cultivar; it and 'Grolau' are particularly good for growing indoors. There are also dwarf and white-flowered forms.

The closely related garlic or Chinese (*Allium tuberosum*) chive has solid, flat leaves to $3/8$ inch wide. These have a mild garlic flavor. The clusters of white flowers are more

open than with chives. There is also a mauve-flowered form.

How to Grow
Light Full sun.
Soil Humus-rich, well-drained soil.
Propagation Sow seeds indoors eight weeks before the last spring frost, placing $1/2$ inch deep. At temperatures between 60° and 70°F, seeds will germinate in two to three

Garlic chives' leaves offer a delicate garlic flavor. The flowers last well in bouquets. Just be sure to remove the faded flowers, as the seeds self-sow.

Chives' mauve flowers are as beautiful as any ornamental, plus they're excellent added to omelettes or other foods, and for flavoring vinegar.

Chive and Blue Cheese Salad Dressing

³/₄ cup buttermilk or non-fat cottage cheese
¹/₄ cup extra-virgin olive oil
3 ounces soft blue cheese, such as Saga or gorgonzola dolce
¹/₄ cup minced fresh chives

Combine all ingredients in a food processor or blender and mix thoroughly until smooth. Serve with any green salad. Makes 1¹/₄ cups. Store remainder in an airtight container in the refrigerator for up to 10 days.

weeks. It's much easier to buy plants in the spring or get a division of about six bulbs from a friend. This should not be too hard, as chives need dividing at least every three years to rejuvenate the clump. You can also divide chives in autumn.

Care Although not absolutely necessary, many gardeners like to stimulate tender fresh new growth by trimming chives back to 2 inches after flowering. To have chives indoors in the winter, start seeds in late summer or dig a small clump in autumn, place it in a container, and leave it outside until the soil freezes; then bring it indoors. Remove the faded flowers of garlic chives to prevent self-sowing.

In the Landscape Think of chives as a low-growing ornamental grass in flower borders, or use them as an edging for beds.

As a companion plant to roses, chives are said to prevent black spot. Along this vein, they may also help deter Japanese beetles, apple scab, peach leaf curl and mildew on cucumbers. More consistently effective is to spray plants with a tea made from the leaves. Chives are also recommended as companion plants for carrots, grapes and tomatoes.

Chives and garlic chives are adaptable to containers filled with a fast-draining potting mix. Feed monthly during the growing season with a balanced fertilizer according to the manufacturer's directions. To extend the season for both chives and garlic chives, over-winter the plants in a cold frame or bring pots indoors.

Culinary Uses

Harvest Cut off leaves at the base any time. Gather flowers just as they open. Preserve by freezing.

In the Kitchen Use chives with vegetables, creamed sauces or egg, cheese, poultry, fish or shellfish dishes. Toss both minced leaves and flowers into salads or make flavored vinegars or butters.

Other Uses

Both the flowers of chives and garlic chives are lovely additions to bouquets or dried for decorating wreaths or other crafts.

Chives have a reputation of repelling insects in the garden; whether true or not, chives definitely add to the garden's flavor.

Few herbs thrive as easily as chives. In fact, chives grow so abundantly that they should be divided at least every three years.

CORIANDER/CILANTRO

Coriandrum sativum
Umbelliferae — carrot family

The name coriander refers to the seeds of this plant, while the foliage goes by cilantro. By whatever name, this is one of the most popular herbs around the world, and has been for much of recorded history. Best of all, not a thing goes wasted: all parts are edible. Besides their use in tomato salsas, the musky-citrusy tasting leaves are an excellent foil for a roasted red pepper soup or a cabbage slaw tossed with an orange vinaigrette. Don't forget to garnish with a sprinkling of the flowers. Try a cilantro pesto made with peanut oil and peanuts. Any combination of the leaves, seeds or roots might be added to a curry sauce with vegetables or spooned over rice. The roots taste like a combination of mild cilantro and celeriac and are a tasty addition to any stir-fry. Or experiment with the orange-spice flavor of the seeds in a marinade for mushrooms. Candied seeds were eaten after Medieval banquets to aid digestion and improve breath odor.

Description
Type Annual.
Size 12 to 18 inches tall, 1 foot wide.
Flowers Flat clusters of tiny, pinkish-white flowers. Summer.
Leaves Rounded and lobed lower leaves resemble flat-leaf parsley; upper leaves are threadlike.
Natural Habitat Native to Mediterranean and southern Europe.
Other Species and Cultivars 'Chinese', Long Standing' and 'Slow Bolt' produce leaves for a longer-than-normal period before flowering.

How to Grow
Light Full sun to light shade.
Soil Humus-rich, moist, well-drained.
Propagation Because the long taproot makes transplanting difficult, it's best to sow seeds directly into the garden in the spring after the last frost. Plant seeds 1/4 inch deep, thinning to 6 inches apart. Make successive sowings at two-week intervals until early summer. Seeds may

Dig up cilantro plants after seed has been produced, and the roots can be cooked and eaten as a vegetable.

also be sown in autumn in Zones 8 to 10.
Care Cilantro grows best in the cool months of spring and autumn. Mulch during the growing season to keep the soil cool and prolong growth. Another way to prolong growth is to remove the flower stalk as soon as it appears.

Choose a variety of cilantro like 'Slow Bolt' to have a supply of leaves for the longest possible period. Even so, make successive sowings about every month.

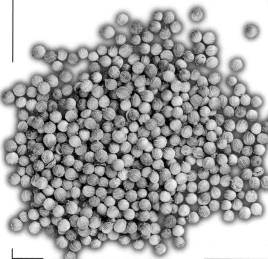

Cilantro undercover: when the seeds are used, the herb is known as coriander.

Start seed of cilantro in pots during the winter in order to have fresh leaves for your Mexican or Asian cooking.

Cucumber and Cilantro Salad

2 medium cucumbers
2 teaspoons salt
1/2 cup plain non-fat yogurt
2 tablespoons fresh cilantro, minced
1 tablespoon fresh chives, minced
1/4 teaspoon freshly ground pepper

Peel and slice the cucumbers and cut into 1/2-inch pieces. Place in a colander and sprinkle with salt. Let them drain for 30 minutes. In a bowl, combine cucumbers, yogurt, cilantro, chives and pepper. Toss gently. Serve immediately or chill. Makes four servings.

In the Landscape Cilantro is often grown in rows in the vegetable garden, to produce an adequate amount of the leaves, seeds and roots. Anise is a good companion plant, but do not grow near fennel.

You can also grow cilantro in containers filled with a fast-draining potting mix. Feed monthly during the growing season with a balanced fertilizer according to the manufacturer's directions. Start seed in pots for growing indoors during the winter.

Culinary Uses

Include the fresh leaves in salsas, salads or marinades. Or stir them in near the end of cooking a stir-fry, rice, grains or pastas. Add the whole or ground seeds to beans, curries, pickles, chutneys, sausage, eggs, cheese or lamb. Desserts also benefit from the seeds—especially stewed fruit, fruit pies, cakes, cookies or sweet quick breads. Flavor vinegar with the leaves, seeds or roots.

Other Uses

Include the orange-scented seeds in potpourris. Drink a tea made from the leaves or seeds for indigestion or to sweeten breath.

Coriander Fruit Crisp

1/4 cup unbleached all-purpose flour
2 tablespoons sugar
2 tablespoons light brown sugar, packed
3 tablespoons butter or margarine, cut into 1/8-inch slices
1 teaspoon coriander seeds, lightly crushed
3 cups fresh or frozen fruit, such as apples, peaches or blueberries
1 tablespoon lemon juice

Preheat oven to 375°F. and butter a 1 1/2-quart baking dish. In a food processor, combine both sugars, flour and butter. Pulse until a cornmeal texture. Add nuts and pulse just until mixed. Do not over-process. Stir in the coriander. Combine the fruit, lemon juice and sugar in the baking dish and sprinkle the flour mixture over the top. Bake for about 45 minutes or until the topping is golden brown. Serve warm or at room temperature. Makes four servings.

These masses of white flowers will soon yield the brown seeds known as coriander, with their orange-spice flavor.

CURRY LEAF

Murraya koenigii
Rutaceae — rue family

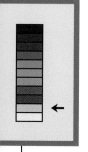

In the tropics of Zone 10 and southwards, curry leaf is an evergreen tropical tree.

Yes, curry powder is a blend of spices. But curry leaf is a subtropical plant whose leaves are often included in curries and other dishes in the cuisines of India, Sri Lanka and throughout Southeast Asia. The somewhat strong, musky scent of the leaves transforms into a pleasant, toasty flavor somewhat like bay when cooked. One of the simplest ways to use the leaves is this: sauté them in oil until they begin to turn brown, add onion and garlic, cook until soft, then add the main ingredient. That ingredient might be vegetables like summer squash or eggplant, tofu, fish or chicken. Don't confuse curry leaf with curry plant (*Helichrysum italicum*), which is a Mediterranean herb with silvery leaves that smell of curry powder.

Description
Type Woody evergreen shrub or tree. Zone 10.
Size 5 to 20 feet tall, 2 to 8 feet wide.

Flowers Clusters of small white flowers. Summer.

Leaves Palm-like fronds of oval, pointed leaves to 2 inches long.

Natural Habitat Native to India and Ceylon.

How to Grow

Light Full sun to light shade.

Soil Humus-rich, moist, well-drained.

Propagation Sow the seed indoors in late winter, placing $1/2$ inch deep with 70°F bottom heat. Older plants send out runners from the underground stems. These can be dug up and repotted. Take cuttings in summer.

Care Be sure to keep the soil evenly moist when growing curry leaf in containers.

In the Landscape Except for those gardens in the warmest climates, curry leaf must be grown in containers and overwintered indoors. Its graceful foliage allows it to be a charming part of a container garden tableau or a featured solo plant. As a container plant, use a fast-draining potting mix and feed monthly with a balanced fertilizer according to the manufacter's directions.

Culinary Uses

Harvest Pick the leaves as you need them. Preserve by freezing. Experiment with drying curry leaf; some people say the flavor is lost, while others recommend it.

In the Kitchen Traditional with lentil, vegetable or meat curries, try curry leaves with other foods by sautéing the leaves with vegetables, adding them to soups or stews, cooking with basmati rice or using them with chutneys, eggs or in a stir-fry.

Like bay, curry leaf has to be grown in containers in most areas of the country.

Other Uses

Drink a tea made from the leaves to relieve digestive problems.

Resembling tiny palm fronds, the evergreen leaves of curry leaf are not a part of curry powder (which is a blend of spices), but the leaves are added to curries.

Mushrooms with Curry Leaf

6 fresh curry leaves, minced
4 scallions, thinly sliced
2 garlic cloves, minced
1 teaspoon minced ginger
2 tablespoons water
1 pound mushrooms, sliced
2 teaspoons curry powder
$1/2$ teaspoon salt
$1/2$ cup unsweetened coconut milk
2 teaspoons lime juice

In a large nonstick skillet, combine curry leaves, scallions, garlic, ginger and water. Cook over medium heat until soft, adding water if necessary. Stir in mushrooms, curry powder and salt. Cook until the mushrooms release their liquid. Reduce heat, cover, then cook for 10 minutes. Stir in the coconut milk and cook, stirring, just until heated. Remove from heat and stir in the lime juice. Serve immediately over jasmine rice. Makes four servings.

DILL

Anethum graveolens
Umbelliferae — carrot family

Most often associated with dill pickles, any number of other vegetables benefit from dill's unique tang. Consider pickling zucchini spears, pearl onions, beets, snap beans, carrots, asparagus spears or okra with dill leaves, flowers or seeds. But don't limit dill just to pickles. The next time you need a quick appetizer, combine some smoked salmon, cream cheese, lemon juice and a dash of cayenne pepper along with some dill leaves in the food processor. Include dill in a chilled cucumber soup or marinated cucumbers. And speaking of marinades, try coating lamb chops with a marinade of yogurt, dill and lemon juice before grilling. However you use it, remember that dill seems to have magical effects on food. The benefits of dill in magicians' spells and lovers'

drinks, as it was used in the Middle Ages, have not been proven.

Description

Type Annual.
Size 18 inches to 4 feet tall, 1 foot wide.
Flowers Flat clusters, to 6 inches across, of tiny yellow flowers. Summer.
Leaves Blue-green, threadlike leaves.
Natural Habitat Native to the Mediterranean and southern Russia.
Other Species and Cultivars Several varieties grow 3 to 4 feet tall and produce foliage for a long periods; these include 'Bouquet', 'Hercules' and 'Tetra Leaf'. For an especially strong flavor and greener leaves, try 'Dukat'. 'Long Island Mammoth' is an heirloom variety with large seedheads. 'Fernleaf' grows only 18 inches tall and produces lots of side branches. 'Vierling' is popular in Europe as a cut flower, but the foliage is also perfectly edible. Indian dill (*A. sowa*), with a more pungent and bitter flavor, is used with steamed rice or soups.

How to Grow

Light Full sun.
Soil Humus-rich, moist, well-drained.
Propagation Sow seed directly into the garden in the spring after

Use dill seeds to give dishes a unique flavor that only dill can provide.

the last frost, thinning to 1 foot apart. For a continuous supply of foliage, sow every three weeks until midsummer.
Care Protect taller types from wind or stake the stems. If

Dill flowers are fragrant and appear in an open head.

Dill's natural blue-green foliage color is intensified in the variety 'Fernleaf', making it an interesting addition to the landscape.

Some people add a head of yellow dill flowers to each jar of pickles, while others prefer to wait until seeds are formed.

Pasta Salad with Vegetables and Dill

2 cups cooked pasta, such as elbows, spirals or bow-ties (start with 1 cup uncooked)
1 cup cooked green peas (fresh or frozen)
1 cup celery, thinly sliced
1/2 cup carrot, grated
1/4 cup scallions, thinly sliced
2 tablespoons fresh dill, minced
1/3 cup mayonnaise
1 tablespoon lemon juice
1 teaspoon sugar
1 teaspoon Dijon mustard
1/2 teaspoon salt
1/4 teaspoon ground black pepper

In a large bowl, combine pasta, peas, celery, carrots, scallions and dill. In a small bowl, combine mayonnaise, lemon juice, sugar, mustard, salt and pepper. Stir the dressing into the vegetables mixture, combining thoroughly. Chill and serve on a bed of lettuce leaves. Makes six servings.

desired, allow at least one plant to self-sow for an early crop next year.

In the Landscape Dill is an ornamental beauty whether planted among herbs, flowers or vegetables. The feathery blue-green foliage and stems, topped with the yellow umbrellas of flowers, add handsome texture and color. In the kitchen garden, dill is a companion plant for cabbage, onions and lettuce.

Dill adapts readily to containers, with 'Fernleaf' being most recommended. Use a fast-draining potting mix and fertilize monthly with a balanced fertilizer according to the manufacturer's directions.

Culinary Uses

Harvest Gather as follows: the leaves as needed; the flowers just as they open; and the seeds when they turn brown, or two or three weeks after blooming. Preserve the leaves by freezing or drying.

In the Kitchen Dill leaves partner well with fish, especially salmon, but also try them with pork, poultry, lamb, cheese, eggs, vegetables, sauces or soups. Or snip some leaves into salads or dips. And don't forget to make some dill butter or vinegar. The best flavor is maintained in dishes that are cooked in a short amount of time or if the dill is added near the end of cooking. Dill seeds have a stronger flavor and are used whole or ground in long-cooked stews, soups or other dishes.

Other Uses

The name dill derives from a Norse word meaning "to lull," and a cup of hot dill tea taken just before bedtime induces a good night's sleep.

Dill's finely cut foliage provides soft texture in the herb garden.

Because 'Fernleaf' dill only grows to 18 inches tall and freely branches, it makes an ideal container plant.

FENNEL

Foeniculum vulgare
Umbelliferae — carrot family

Uncooked, fennel brings a soft, nutty version of anise or licorice to food. With cooking, it mellows into a unique sweetness all its own. Whichever way, fennel is a fish herb *par excellance*. Stuff a whole fish with the leaves before poaching or grilling, include leaves in a sauce for serving with fish, or toss dried stems on the coals of the grill. Stems and seeds are also edible, and all parts of fennel may also flavor a wide range of other foods. Fennel is one of the oldest cultivated plants, with Roman soldiers eating it for strength while the women used it as a way to stay thin. The Anglo-Saxons considered it one of the nine sacred herbs with power over evil.

Description

Type Perennial. Zone 6 to 9.

Size 4 to 6 feet tall, 18 inches wide.

Flowers Flat clusters of tiny yellow flowers to 6 inches across. Summer.

Leaves Threadlike, feathery, blue-green leaves.

Natural Habitat Native to the Mediterranean. Widely naturalized.

Other Species and Cultivars
Bronze fennel (*F. vulgare* 'purpurascens') has mild-tasting, purplish-brown foliage.
Florence fennel (*F. vulgare* var. *azoricum*), also known as bulb

Fennel closely resembles dill in appearance, but the flavor is more allied to anise.

or sweet fennel and finocchio, is an annual vegetable with a swollen, white leaf base.

How to Grow

Light Full sun.

Soil Humus-rich, moist, well-drained.

Propagation Sow seed directly into the garden in spring about two weeks before the last frost, thinning to 18 inches apart.

Care A bonus with fennel is that the nectar of the flowers draws swallowtail butterflies to the garden. Don't be alarmed when you see the green-black-and-yellow-striped caterpillars of these butterflies. Just grow enough fennel for both you and them.

In the Landscape Fennel's height lends stately form to the back of the border, and it is especially striking planted in back of pink-flowered cosmos and white shasta daisies. Bronze fennel's purplish foliage provides drama anywhere in the garden, but par-

ticularly with brightly colored flowers such as orange and red zinnias, dahlias and nasturtiums, plus golden calendulas.

Do not plant fennel near bush beans, caraway, coriander, kohlrabi, tomatoes or wormwood, as they adversely affect each other.

Dark brown fennel seeds have long been eaten after a meal as an aid to digestion.

Chilled Beet Soup with Fennel

8 ounces beets, cooked and peeled
3 cups vegetable stock or broth
1 tablespoon lemon juice
1/2 teaspoon fennel seed, lightly crushed
1 teaspoon sugar
1/2 teaspoon salt
1/4 teaspoon ground black pepper
2 large hard-boiled eggs, diced
1/2 cup peeled, seeded and diced cucumber
2 scallions, thinly sliced
1/2 cup sour cream
1/4 cup minced fresh fennel leaves

In a blender, combine beets, stock or broth, lemon juice, fennel seed, sugar, salt and pepper. Blend thoroughly. Chill. Stir in eggs, cucumber and scallions. Pour into individual bowls. Top each with a dollop of sour cream and sprinkle with the fennel leaves. Serve immediately. Makes four servings.

Bronze fennel, with its purplish-brown and fine-textured leaves, becomes indispensable in the landscape once you begin to see the effect it adds.

Those who grow fennel are in good company. None other than Winston Churchill kept a caged garden of fennel at his estate in Chartwell, England, in order to raise swallowtail butterflies.

Fennel makes a dramatic centerpiece for a mixed container planting. Use a fast-draining potting mix and fertilize monthly during the growing season with a balanced fertilizer according to the manufacturer's directions. Overwinter outdoors in a sheltered spot and mulch around the container.

Culinary Uses
Harvest Gather leaves at any time or the seeds just as they turn from yellowish-green to brown. Preserve the leaves by freezing.
In the Kitchen Add the leaves to salads, dips, sauces, marinades, butters and vinegars. Pair them with fish, eggs, cheese, vegetables or rice. Eat the stems fresh or cooked like celery. Include the whole or ground seeds in sausage, cakes, cookies, breads or fruit desserts.

Other Uses
Drink a tea of fennel leaves or seeds for indigestion or to suppress the appetite. The tea can also be used as a facial tonic.

The stems of bulb or Florence fennel become swollen at the base and are eaten as a vegetable. Use the foliage like the herb fennel.

Fennel's light, airy look contrasts well with bold, coarser-leafed plants.

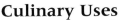

GARLIC

Allium sativum
Liliaceae — lily family

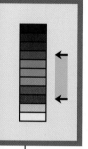

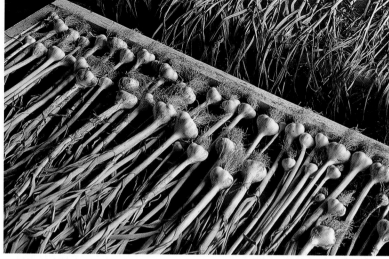

After digging garlic, spread the plants out on trays in a dark, dry, well-ventilated place for several days.

Grown and relished since earliest recorded time, garlic was thought to possess magical powers as well as the ability to improve strength and endurance. It has been prescribed as a medicine since pre-Biblical times. Modern research has proven it to assist with inhibiting blood clotting, decreasing blood cholesterol and triglycerides, improving resistance to cancer, and removing heavy metals in our bodies. It also has antiseptic, antibacterial and antifungal properties. In cooking, the pungent, intense flavor is found around the world in all foods except dessert (although there are those who swear you can do that, too).

Description
Type Perennial bulb. Zones 4 to 9.

Size 2 feet tall, 8 inches wide.
Flowers Globe-shaped, 2-inch cluster of small white flowers.
Leaves Strap-shaped leaves to $^1/_2$ inch wide and 10 inches long.
Natural Habitat Unknown, but possibly southern Siberia.

Once dry, cut or twist off the tops and the bulbs are ready to enjoy fresh, cooked or roasted.

Other Species and Cultivars
Garlic is divided into two categories, hardneck and softneck. Hardneck types, so-called because the flower stem dries hard in the center of the bulb, tend to have fewer cloves, more pungent flavor and thicker and more easily peeled skins, but a shelf life of only three to four months. Some of the varieties to look for include 'Spanish Roja', 'French Red Rocambole', 'German White', 'Carpathian' and 'German Red'. The softneck types have more cloves and a milder flavor, plus they can be stored for up to a year. Among the varieties of softneck are 'California Early', 'Silverskin', 'Polish White', 'Inchelium', 'Machashi' and 'Early Red Italian'. Elephant garlic, which is actually a type of leek, has a flower stalk like a hardneck garlic, a mild garlic flavor, four to six very large, easy to peel cloves in each bulb, and stores well.

How to Grow
Light Full sun.
Soil Humus-rich, moist, well-drained.
Propagation Although you can start garlic from seed, it is much easier to plant individual cloves. Plant the cloves 2 inches deep and 4 inches apart, four to six weeks before the first frost in autumn. Use only the larger cloves. The smaller ones can be eaten or planted in a separate area, spacing 2 inches apart for spring baby garlic (which is eaten like scallions). Plant elephant garlic cloves 4 inches deep.

Garlic is also easily grown in containers, provided there is good drainage.

For those who really love garlic, growing your own gives you the opportunity to plant large blocks in the garden.

Plant individual cloves about 4 inches apart and 2 inches deep, preferably four to six weeks before the first frost in autumn.

Roasted Garlic

Preheat oven to 300°F. Cut off the top ¼-inch of an entire garlic bulb. Place it in a garlic roaster, ramekin or on a square of aluminum foil. Pour a tablespoon or so of liquid (such as vegetable broth, wine, brandy or vinegar) over the top. Sprinkle on some fresh herbs (such as rosemary, sage, thyme or oregano) if desired. Cover the roaster or ramekin or seal the foil. Bake for about 1 hour or until soft. Let cool until easily handled, then squeeze the garlic into a small bowl. If not eaten immediately, store in the refrigerator. You can also "roast" garlic in the microwave by placing it in a covered microwave-safe bowl and cooking it on high for about 4 minutes. Let stand for 5 minutes.

Care Apply several inches of mulch in late autumn. Remove the flower stalks in the spring or early summer so that all the plant's energy goes into the developing bulb.

In the Landscape Garlic is usually planted in rows in the kitchen garden, but you can also plant groups of six or eight bulbs in the herb or flower garden. Garlic is a good companion plant for roses, cabbage, eggplant, tomatoes and fruit trees.

Culinary Uses

Harvest Autumn-planted cloves are ready for harvest the following summer. Bulbs are ready to be dug up (don't pull) when the lower leaves have turned brown. Place the newly dug plants on a screen in a dark, dry, well-ventilated place for several days, then shake off the soil. Cut or twist off the tops. Store the bulbs in a dark, cool, dry, well-ventilated location.

In the Kitchen Garlic enlivens eggs, cheese, beef, pork, poultry, fish, vegetables, salads, salad dressings, vinegars, soups, stews, pastas, stir-fries, sauces, butters, marinades and vinegars. Pickle garlic to add to a relish tray or martini. Use roasted garlic as a soft, mellow, nutty spread for crackers or toast, or stir it into mashed potatoes.

Other Uses

Eat raw garlic or steep several chopped cloves in hot water or broth for colds, flu, sore throats or general health, as cooking garlic tends to reduce its medicinal effectiveness. To combat garlic breath, eat fresh parsley, cardamom seeds or strawberries afterwards. Make a spray to control aphids by soaking some of the cloves in water.

Hardneck garlic has a more pungent flavor than soft-necked, but it also has a shorter shelf life, lasting only three or four months in storage.

GINGER

Zingiber officinale
Zingiberaceae — ginger family

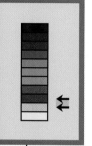

In tropical climates, ginger plants can grow to 4 or more feet tall.

With its lemon-spice tang, ginger adapts to both sweet and savory foods. A stir-fry seldom begins without first cooking a quarter-sized piece in oil, and administering ginger ale for an upset stomach is further testament to the herb's soothing qualities.

The branching, knobby rhizomes (underground stems) have a smooth, pale ocher skin and palest yellow flesh, which becomes fibrous with age. Seldom is the juicy young ginger available, so the only way to have it is by growing it in your garden. Fresh ginger is most often found in the cuisines of China, India, Japan, Southeast Asia, North Africa and the Caribbean.

Description

Type Perennial. Zones 9 to 10.
Size 2 to 4 feet tall, 1 foot wide.
Flowers Dense, conelike, 3-inch spikes with 1-inch yellow and purple flowers, but rarely flowers in cultivation.
Leaves Pointed, strap-shaped leaves, 6 to 12 inches long and 3/4 inch wide.
Natural Habitat Native to southern China and India.
Other Species and Cultivars Japanese ginger (*Z. mioga*) has a bergamot-like flavor. Ginger is closely related to both the greater and lesser galangals and turmeric.

How to Grow

Light Light shade.
Soil Humus-rich, moist, well-drained.
Propagation Start a pot of ginger from a section of rhizome, such as those sold at grocery stores, laying it flat and 1 inch deep in a container of fast-draining potting soil in early spring. Keep indoors until all danger of frost is past.
Care Ginger grows best with heat and humidity, and the

Carrots with Ginger and Cardamom

1 pound baby carrots, peeled
3 tablespoons butter or margarine
1 tablespoon minced fresh ginger
1 teaspoon ground cardamom seed
1 clove garlic, finely minced
2 tablespoons lemon juice

In a saucepan fitted with a steamer, cook carrots for 5 to 8 minutes or until tender. Drain and set aside. In a nonstick skillet, melt the butter over medium heat. Stir in the ginger, cardamom and garlic. Sauté for 1 minute. Stir in the carrots and lemon juice. Heat through. Serve immediately. Makes four servings.

nades, jams, chutneys, quick breads, muffins, cakes, cookies or fruit desserts. It goes especially well with pork, poultry, fish and yellow vegetables such as winter squash, sweet potatoes and carrots.

Other Uses

Make a tea from the rhizome, adding honey and lemon, if desired, for colds, flu, sore throat, indigestion, nausea or motion sickness.

soil kept evenly moist. Foliage goes dormant in the autumn.

In the Landscape In climates colder than Zone 9, ginger is usually grown in containers, where it makes an attractive foliage plant. Feed monthly during the growing season with a balanced fertilizer according to the manufacturer's directions.

Culinary Uses

Harvest After at least eight months of growth, pull the plants out of the container, cut off the leafstalks and remove the fibrous roots. Wash and dry the rhizomes. There are two ways to preserve ginger. One is to peel the rhizomes, cut them into 1-inch pieces, put them in a glass jar, cover them with vodka and store in the refrigerator. The other is to wrap the rhizomes in a paper towel, then in an airtight container and store in the refrigerator.

In the Kitchen You can slice, chop, shred, grate or mince fresh ginger and add it to any stir-fry, soups, braised or steamed dishes, mari-

You can start your own ginger plants from a rhizome bought at the grocery store.

HORSERADISH

Armoracia rusticana
Cruciferae — mustard family

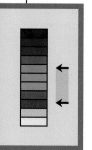

Horseradish plants have large, bold foliage that spreads rapidly, so choose their location carefully.

excellent foil to a variety of foods.

Description

Type Perennial. Zones 5 to 9.
Size 2 to 3 feet tall, each plant 1 foot wide, but quickly sends up new plants.
Flowers Clusters of small white flowers.
Leaves Strap-shaped, wavy-edged leaves to 1 foot long.
Natural Habitat Native to eastern Europe and western Asia.
Other Species and Cultivars 'Variegata' has green-and-white leaves.

Calling horseradish pungent verges on being an understatement. Sinus-clearing might be more appropriate. Perhaps it's not surprising then that for centuries horseradish was considered a medicine rather than a condiment. By the Middle Ages, Germans and Danes had appropriated it for the dinner table. The French and English did not adopt it until the 17th century. Since then a paste of grated horseradish root and vinegar have become synonymous with roast beef. For a more refined effect, add a bit of the grated root to mayonnaise or a cream sauce. In whatever form, the mustard nature of horseradish provides an

How to Grow

Light Full sun.
Soil Deep, humus-rich, moist, well-drained.
Propagation Horseradish is most often started by planting young roots about 8 inches long and $1/2$ inch wide. Set 1 foot apart and 6 inches deep in early spring or autumn. You can also start plants directly from seed, sowing into the garden

To use the roots, scrape off the brown peel and grate the white part.

about 2 weeks before the last frost.

Care The best roots form in deeply prepared soil with no stones.

In the Landscape You might want to choose an isolated spot for horseradish, as it spreads rapidly. One way to contain it is by planting in a bottomless 5-gallon container sunken into the soil. Horseradish is considered a companion plant for potatoes.

Apple and Horseradish Relish

1 large apple
1/4 cup low-fat or non-fat sour cream
2 tablespoons lemon juice
2 tablespoons grated horseradish
1 teaspoon Dijon mustard
1 teaspoon sugar

Peel, core and grate apples into a bowl. Add lemon juice, horseradish, mustard and sugar. Combine thoroughly. Store in an airtight container in the refrigerator for up to two weeks. Serve as a condiment with poultry, beef or fish. Makes 3/4 cup.

Culinary Uses

Harvest Dig up horseradish roots in late autumn, continuing until the ground freezes. To store, pack the scrubbed roots in a container of dry sand kept in a cool, dark place. Or keep them in the refrigerator crisper drawer. When ready to use, peel the roots.

In the Kitchen Horseradish enhances smoked fish, sausage, beef, beets, potato salad, slaw, poached fish or poultry. Add a few of the very youngest, most tender leaves to a tossed green salad.

Other Uses

A poultice of horseradish root is an old-fashioned remedy for sore muscles. Be careful—using too much for too long can blister the skin.

Horseradish roots are usually dug up in the fall until the ground freezes.

Horseradish flowers are edible and lend a delicate version of the pungent root flavor to salads.

HYSSOP

Hyssopus officinalis
Labiatae — mint family

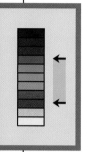

In cooking, a little bit of hyssop can go a long way, what with the strong flavor combining camphor and mint. Still, hyssop is not to be overlooked. Besides its affinity with fatty foods like lamb or duck, hyssop is splendid with all types of fruits. Scholars aren't sure if this is the same hyssop mentioned in the Bible, but this herb is known for its ability to calm an upset stomache or soothe skin. Most important, perhaps, is the beauty hyssop brings to the garden with its fine-textured, dark, evergreen leaves and spires of tiny dark blue-violet flowers from midsummer until autumn. An added bonus is the bounty of bees, butterflies and hummingbirds that the hyssop flowers lure to the landscape.

Description
Type Perennial. Zones 4 to 9.
Size 1 to 3 feet tall, 3 feet across.
Flowers Dense, whorled spikes of $1/2$-inch blue to violet flowers.
Leaves Lance-shaped, evergreen leaves to $1^1/2$ inches long and $1/4$ inch wide.
Natural Habitat Native to Europe and Asia.
Other Species and Cultivars There are forms with pink or white flowers. Rock hyssop (*H. officinalis* subsp. *aristatus*) grows 1 foot tall.

How to Grow
Light Full sun to light shade.
Soil Humus-rich, well-drained.
Propagation Sow seed directly into the garden, $1/4$ inch deep, one or two weeks before the last frost in spring. Thin to 1 foot apart. Take cuttings in summer or divide hyssop in spring or autumn.
Care Hyssop needs very little care except to trim off the faded flowers and shape the plants as needed.
In the Landscape Hyssop has multiple personalities in the garden. If only minimally

Hyssop is clearly related to oregano—both are attractive in the garden.

Besides the blue-flowering form, hyssop also comes with pink or white flowers.

Folklore holds that hyssop repels flea beetles and lures cabbage moths away from cabbage family members.

Hyssop is a worthy addition to the container garden. Use a fast-draining potting mix and feed monthly during the growing season with a balanced fertilizer according to the manufacturer's directions. Overwinter outdoors in a protected spot, mulching around the container.

The flavor of hyssop blends mint and camphor. Hyssop is especially good with fruit, lamb stews and roasted duck.

trimmed, the plants casually soften the edges of beds or borders. Or, you can clip hyssop frequently as a very low, formal hedge, perhaps as part of a knot garden. Hyssop is especially complementary to a planting of roses.

Culinary Uses

Harvest Gather young stems of hyssop and gently strip off the leaves or flowers. Preserve by drying.

In the Kitchen Both the leaves and flowers enhance green or fruit salads, stock or broth, lentil soup, fruit soups, fruit desserts, pork or lamb stews, poultry stuffings, homemade liqueurs, butters or vinegars.

Combine with mint or lemon balm for a refreshing tea.

Other Uses

Include the fresh flowers in bouquets, or the dried leaves or flowers in potpourri. Drink a cup of tea made from the leaves for indigestion, cough or a sore throat. Or use hyssop in bathwater or as a facial steam to soothe and cleanse skin.

Fresh Peaches with Hyssop

1 cup orange juice
2 tablespoons sugar
2 teaspoons minced fresh hyssop leaves
4 peaches
³/4 cup whipped cream or whipped topping
2 tablespoons fresh hyssop flowers
2 tablespoons pecans, toasted and chopped

In a small bowl, combine orange juice, sugar and hyssop. Peel, halve, pit and slice the peaches. Place the peaches in a shallow dish and pour the orange juice mixture over the top. Cover and refrigerate. To serve, divide the peaches between four small bowls. Put a dollop of cream or topping on each one, then garnish with the flowers and pecans. Serve immediately. Makes four servings.

Lush growth, fine-textured leaves and lasting flowers make hyssop a good ornamental, particularly as an edging, because it can be sheared.

KAFFIR LIME

Citrus hystrix
Rutaceae — rue family

Kaffir lime brings a fresh, citrus flavor to many foods.

The leaves of kaffir lime are unusual in that they are divided crosswise in the middle. Regardless of form, the citrus flavor is wonderful.

As Southeast Asian cuisine has increased in popularity, so has the kaffir lime. It is the leaves, not the fruit, that most often brings a lemony tang to the foods of Thailand, Vietnam, Cambodia, Indonesia and Malaysia. Nearly every Thai soup is flavored with kaffir lime leaves, and they also find their way into stir-fries or curries. Frequently, they are paired with garlic, ginger, hot peppers and Thai basil for seasoning a dish. The fruits yield very little juice, but both fruit and rind are used in curry pastes. The fragrance of the juice is said to ward off evil spirits.

Description

Type Woody shrub or small tree. Zones 10 to 11.

Size 5 to 15 feet tall, 2 to 5 feet wide.

Flowers Waxy, white, 1-inch across. Intermittent.

Leaves Oval, pointed, leathery, bright green leaves that are

Kaffir limes are fun plants for containers.

Thai Vegetable Soup

4 cups vegetable stock or broth
2 fresh kaffir lime leaves
1 stalk fresh lemon grass, trimmed back to the white base and minced
4 scallions, thinly sliced
¼ pound fresh spinach, washed and trimmed
½ pound bok choy, cut crosswise in ¹/₂-inch slices
¼ pound shiitake mushrooms, stemmed and sliced
1 teaspoon soy sauce
2 cups cooked jasmine rice
2 tablespoons minced fresh cilantro leaves

In a large saucepan, combine the stock or broth and the lime leaves. Place over medium-high heat. Lower heat when liquid begins to simmer. Continue cooking for 5 minutes. Stir in the lemon grass and scallions and simmer for another 5 minutes.

Tear the spinach leaves into pieces and add to the pan along with the mushrooms, bok choy and soy sauce. Simmer for 5 minutes. Place the hot jasmine rice in large bowl and pour the soup around it. Garnish with the cilantro and serve immediately. Makes four servings.

notched in the middle, so that they look like two leaves.

Natural Habitat
Naturalized in Southeast Asia.

How to Grow

Light Full sun.

Soil Humus-rich, moist, well-drained.

Propagation Cuttings in spring or summer.

Care If leaves start to turn yellow, apply a fertilizer containing chelated iron, zinc and manganese. Spray scale with horticultural soap.

In the Landscape Shiny foliage, beautiful blooms and lovely fruit combine to make the thorny kaffir lime a conversation piece in the garden. Because of its susceptibility to cold temperatures, most people will want to grow kaffir lime in a container and bring it indoors in winter. Use a fast-draining potting soil and fertilize monthly with a balanced fertilizer according to the manufacturer's directions. Allow the top ¹/₂ inch of soil to dry out before watering.

Culinary Uses

Harvest You can pick the leaves year-round. Preserve by freezing. Pick the fruit when still green or as it yellows, using the rind fresh or dried as well as the juice.

In the Kitchen Add the whole leaves at the beginning of cooking curries, soups, stir-fries or stews made with poultry, tofu, tempeh or seafood. Remove the leaves before serving.

Other Uses

Make a tea from the leaves for a fragrant hair rinse.

For large houseplants, consider growing kaffir lime with bay.

LAVENDER

Lavandula species and cultivars
Labiatae — mint family

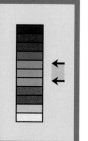

Gray foliage and masses of purple flower spikes will entice you to plant lavender throughout your garden.

It might be a surprise to find lavender among culinary herbs, but this sweetly-scented cottage garden favorite has been used to flavor foods since ancient times. Lavender ice cream most often appears on the menus at trendy restaurants, but the flowers and leaves are also delicious in all sorts of baked goods and they are a surprisingly good partner with main-course egg dishes. Lavender jelly is a tea-time treat, perhaps served with blueberry muffins. Of course, lavender flowers are best known for their presence in sachets to scent linen and lingerie as well as to prevent moths. The dried flower stems are also used in arrangements and other fragrant crafts. A bit of lavender tea dabbed on the temples or applied as a compress readily relieves stress or a headache. All this and the plants are lovely in the garden too.

Description
Type The most common types are evergreen, woody perennials. Zones 5 to 8. There are

French lavender offers leaves with scalloped edges. Only hardy to Zone 9, other gardeners can grow it as an annual or in pots brought indoors in winter.

Lavender is a classic herb, both in the kitchen and garden.

also tender species often grown as annuals.

Size 8 inches to 3 feet tall, 1 to 4 feet wide.

Flowers 6- to 12-inch long leafless stalks with tightly spaced whorls of small, lavender-colored flowers. Summer.

Leaves Lance-shaped, gray-green leaves to 2 inches long and 1/4 inch wide.

Natural Habitat Native to the Mediterranean.

Other Species and Cultivars
The most popular and commonly grown lavender is English lavender (*L. angustifolia*), which at various times has been botanically labeled *L. officinalis, L. angustifolius, L. vera, L. spica, L. pyrenaica* and *L. delphinensis*. The favored cultivars are 'Hidcote', with deep purple flowers and 'Munstead', with lavender-blue flowers; both grow between 8 and 12 inches tall and wide. There are also pink- and white-flowered forms, plus a number of others in various shades of purplish-blue.

'Grosso' and 'Provence' (*L. X intermedia*) are two widely grown cultivars that are hybrids between *L. angustifolia* and *L. latifolia* . They have a more camphorous scent and flavor than English lavender. These grow 8 to 16 inches tall and spread up to 3 feet. They are hardy in Zones 6 to 8.

From the dozens of other species and cultivars, consider Spanish lavender (*L. stoechas*), with large, showy flower bracts; French lavender (*L. dentata*), with scalloped-edge leaves; and green lavender (*L. viridis*) with green flowers. Fernleaf lavender (*L. multifida*) and jagged lavender (*L. pinnata*) have similar lacy, velvety foliage and are often confused in the trade. All of these are hardy at least in Zone 9, or they may be grown as annuals. Spike lavender (*L. latifolia*) has resinous-scented foliage and is hardy to Zone 7.

How to Grow
Light Full sun.
Soil Humus-rich, well-drained.

Propagation Because most of lavender's cultivars do not come true from seed, and the seed is very slow to germinate, lavender is seldom started from seed. The exception is the cultivar 'Lavender Lady', which was expressly bred for starting from seed; sow it indoors eight weeks before the last frost in spring. Plant lavenders into the garden after all frost danger is past, spacing 1 to 3 feet apart depending on mature height. Take cuttings in summer from the side shoots, place in a cold frame and grow there for a year before transplanting to the garden. It's somewhat easier to layer lavender in summer.

Care Lavenders need good air circulation around them, which helps prevent fungal diseases. Trim plants the first year after planting to prevent flowering and to encourage branching. Thereafter, prune after flowering and again in the spring to remove any dead wood; never cut into old wood, as it will not sprout new growth. Good soil drainage is especially important during the winter, and the pH should be 7.0.

In the Landscape Lavender makes a spectacular low hedge. Placed along a walk, it is easy to brush up against and delight in the scent. Even if you have just a few plants, place them within easy reach.

Lavenders grow very well in containers and also can be trained into standards. Use a fast-draining potting mix and feed monthly during the growing season with a balanced fertilizer according to the manufacturer's directions. If you bring the pots indoors in the winter, provide bright light and daytime temperatures of 50 to 60°F.

Culinary Uses

Harvest Pick the stems of lavender flowers anytime from when they just begin to open to until they are fully open. Preserve by drying, removing the dried flowers from the stems. The fresh flower petals have the sweetest flavor. Lavender foliage can substitute for the flowers, using half as much; lavender makes a good substitute for rosemary, using twice as much lavender as rosemary.

In the Kitchen Crystallize the flowers for decorating pastries or add them to cakes, cookies, fruit desserts, omelettes, quiches, jellies, butters or vinegars. Throw the lavender

Along with 'Hidcote', 'Munstead' is one of the most popular of the English lavenders.

Inhaling the fragrance of lavender relieves stress, while adding the flowers to desserts fulfills the sweet tooth.

'Nana', or dwarf English lavender, forms a compact mound less than a foot tall when in bloom.

stems on the charcoal in the grill to flavor grilled food.

Other Uses

Use the stems of fresh lavender in bouquets. Stems of the dried flowers are lovely in crafts, wreaths or arrangements. Remove the flowers from the stems and include them in potpourris, moth-repellent sachets, incense or sleep or eye pillows. When dining outdoors, rub the flowers on your skin to repel flies. Drink a tea made from the flowers for tension or headaches. Or, use the tea in bathwater, facial tonics, hair rinses or a cold compress for headaches.

Lavender Cookies

¹/₂ cup (1 stick or 4 ounces) butter, at room temperature
¹/₂ cup sugar
1 large egg
1 tablespoon fresh or dried lavender flowers
1 cup unbleached all-purpose flour
1 teaspoon baking powder

Preheat oven to 350°F. In a bowl, cream butter and sugar until light and fluffy. Add the egg and lavender, then beat well. Slowly stir in the flour and baking powder, combining well. Drop by tablespoonfuls onto a baking sheet sprayed with non-stick cooking spray or lined with baking parchment, leaving 2 inches between the cookies. Bake for 15 to 20 minutes or until golden. Remove and cool on a wire rack. Store in an airtight container. Makes two dozen cookies.

Although an obvious contradiction, white lavender has its own particular charms, especially when combined with woolly thyme along a walk.

LEMON BALM

Melissa officinalis
Labiatae — mint family

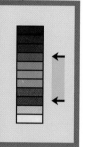

Lemon balm has a refreshing lemon fragrance and flavor with an underlying quality of mint. It is at its best when added to uncooked food, such as salads, or stirred in near the end of cooking. But don't hesitate to stuff a whole fish with lemon balm before baking or grilling, then remove the leaves before serving. Lemon balm's heritage traces back to the Roman scholar Pliny, who noted that bees preferred it this gave rise to the genus name, which is the Latin word for bees. Moving forward, medieval Arab physicians recommend it for lifting the spirits, and 17th-century herbalists wrote that it "causeth the mind and heart to become merry." Indeed, lemon balm tea does seem to have a calming effect.

has bright yellow foliage; grow in light shade as full sun may scorch the leaves.

Another lemon-flavored herb in the mint family is Vietnamese balm (*Elsholtzia ciliata*). It is an annual that grows 3 feet tall and has oval, pointed, toothed leaves to 3 inches long and 1 inch wide. It has a flavor similar to lemon balm, but with more of a minty taste; it can also withstand cooking better.

How to Grow

Light Full sun to light shade.
Soil Humus-rich, moist, well-drained.

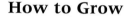

To keep the leaves of golden lemon balm from scorching, grow it in light shade.

Propagation Sow seeds outdoors after all danger of frost is past in spring. Barely cover the seeds and keep moist until they germinate. Thin to 2 feet apart. Take cuttings or

Description

Type Perennial. Zones 4 to 9.
Size 2 feet tall, 2 feet wide.
Flowers Small clusters of $1/2$-inch white flowers. Summer.
Leaves Heart-shaped, deeply veined leaves with scalloped edges.
Natural Habitat Native to Southern Europe and North Africa.
Other Species and Cultivars 'Aurea', also listed as 'Variegata', has green leaves splashed with gold. 'Allgold'

Lemon balm closely resembles it relative, mint, in appearance. But the fragrance is pure lemon. Just don't let it go to seed!

Lemon balm has a reputation in the kitchen as well as in some old medicines.

Lemon Bulgur

2 tablespoons canola oil
1/2 cup finely chopped onion
1/2 cup finely chopped celery
1 cup bulgur
2 cups vegetable stock or broth
1/2 cup minced, fresh lemon balm

In a saucepan, warm the oil over medium-low heat. Stir in the onion and celery and cook, stirring for 3 minutes. Stir in the bulgur and cook, stirring for another 2 minutes. Add the stock or broth, bring to a boil, reduce heat, cover and simmer for 20 minutes or until the bulgur is tender and the liquid is absorbed. Stir in lemon balm and serve immediately. Makes four servings.

layer in spring or summer or divide in spring or autumn.

Care It may take a year for plants to reach their stride. Trim back faded flowers before seed sets to keep the plants from self-sowing.

In the Landscape Lemon balm brings a fresh, bright green color to the garden. The golden forms bring sparkle to lightly shaded beds or borders, providing textural contrast with variegated hostas, for instance.

Lemon balm easily grows in containers filled with a fast-draining potting mix and a monthly feeding with a balanced fertilizer according to the manufacturer's directions. Bring the plants inside during the winter or overwinter them outdoors in a protected place with a mulch around the pots.

Culinary Uses

Harvest For small quantities, gather lemon balm leaves as you need them. The best time for a large harvest is just before the plants bloom, cutting the plants back to 2 inches. Preserve by drying, although some of the scent is lost. Foliage may turn black if it is not dried quickly at about 100°F.

In the Kitchen Add fresh lemon balm leaves to salads, including tossed, fruit, bean, pasta, chicken, potato or tuna. Use them in marinades for fish, vegetables or olives. Make butters for corn-on-the-cob, broccoli, asparagus or green beans. Flavor yogurt, vinegars, liqueur or wine. Steep the leaves in sugar syrup for cooking with fruit.

Other Uses

Place a bouquet of the leaves on the outdoor dining table to repel insects. In a nosegay, lemon balm signifies sympathy. Rub some of the fresh leaves on wood furniture for a lemon-scented polish. Use the dried leaves as a base for potpourris or in herb pillows. Drink a tea made from the leaves for stress, tension, insomnia, indigestion or headaches. Dab some of the tea for relief on cuts or insect stings or add it to bathwater or facial steams.

Variegated lemon balm may revert to solid green in summer. Cut it back to the ground and the new foliage will once more be dappled.

LEMON GRASS

Cymbopogon citratus
Gramineae — grass family

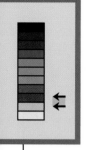

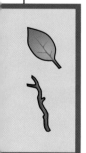

Provide bright light and even watering, and your lemon grass will be part of tantalizing dishes and soothing herb teas all winter.

several crushed stems to vegetable stock or broth.

Description
Type Perennial. Zones 9 to 10.
Size 3 to 5 feet tall, 4 feet wide.
Flowers Inconspicuous green flowers on long stalks. Seldom flowers.
Leaves Slender, arching, light green, grass-like leaves.
Natural Habitat Native to Southeast Asia.
Other Species and Cultivars Rose grass (*C. martinii*) offers leaves with the scent of roses. East Indian lemon grass (*C. flexuosus*) is commercialy used as a food flavoring. Citronella (*C. nardus*) is grown for citronella oil.

How to Grow
Light Full sun.
Soil Humus-rich, moist, well-drained soil.
Propagation Sow seeds indoors six weeks before the last frost in spring. Plant outdoors after

With the influx of herbs from around the world in the last decade or so, lemon grass has won the "most popular" title. The fat, fibrous stalks hold the lemon-scented oils that make it a tantalizing ingredient in Southeast Asian dishes as well as others. To cook with lemon grass, cut off the upper leafy section and remove the outer leaf sheaths of the leaf bases until reaching the inner white part. Cut this white part into 2- or 3-inch sections. Crush these with the back of a knife or mallet and remove them before the dish is served, as you would with bay leaves. Or thinly slice, chop or pound them into a paste and keep in the dish. A simple way to experience cooking with lemon grass is to add

It is the fleshy lower stems of lemon grass that are most commonly used in cooking.

Why grow an ornamental grass that you can't eat? Lemon grass is pretty and it flavors food too!

the last frost, spacing 2 to 4 feet apart or plant in containers. Divide in spring or early summer, trimming the leaves to 4 inches long.

Care Lemon grass is very easy to grow, although cats may nibble on the leaves or dig the plant up. If you don't want to overwinter lemon grass indoors, simply treat it as an annual.

In the Landscape Lemon grass brings graceful, grassy foliage to the garden. It is dramatic when situated in the garden where the sun shines through the leaves. Be warned in siting it—the leaves have sharp edges, so it's not a plant to be brushed against.

Because lemon grass does not withstand freezing temperatures, most gardeners grow it in containers filled with a fast-draining potting mix and a monthly fertilizing with a balanced fertilizer according to the manufacturer's directions. Overwinter indoors in bright light.

Culinary Uses

Harvest Remove older outside stems when about $1/2$ inch thick, breaking or cutting off at the base. Harvest young leaves for tea. Keep the stems wrapped and stored in the refrigerator for up to two weeks or preserve for up to a year by freezing.

In the Kitchen Finely mince the white bulbous lower stem and use in Southeast Asian dishes including curries, beef, chicken, fish stews, stir-fries, pasta, soups, syrups or hot or cold tea.

Other Uses

Break up the dried leaves and add them to potpourris. Drink a tea made from the leaves to relieve tension, headaches or indigestion.

Shrimp and Lemon Grass Soup

1 fresh or dried chili pepper
1 stalk fresh lemon grass, trimmed back to white base
4 cups vegetable stock or broth
1 pound medium shrimp, peeled and de-veined
2 tablespoons lemon juice
4 scallions, thinly sliced
2 tablespoons minced fresh cilantro leaves

Put the pepper and lemon grass into a muslin cooking bag or tie into a piece of cheesecloth. Place this with the stock or broth in a large saucepan. Place over medium-high heat and bring to a boil. Reduce heat to low, cover and simmer for 20 minutes. Remove the cover, add the shrimp and simmer for 5 to 8 minutes or until the shrimp are done. Stir in lemon juice and scallions and cook until heated through. Remove the pepper and lemon grass, pour into four bowls and garnish with the cilantro. Serve immediately. Makes four servings.

Because it is only hardy to Zone 9, gardeners sometimes grow lemon grass in pots that can be brought indoors in winter.

LEMON VERBENA

Aloysia triphylla
Verbenaceae — verbena family

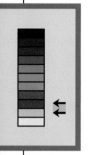

Enjoy lemon verbena's citrus flavor by keeping the plants bushy and full. Regularly pinch out the branches' growing tips.

Spanish explorers, Scarlet O'Hara's mother and Victorian ladies have all been charmed by the sweet lemon scent of lemon verbena. For many years it was more popular in perfumes and commercial soaps, cosmetics and bath oils than in the kitchen. Yet with a little experimentation, you should find all manner of ways that it can brighten the flavors in foods. Put some leaves in the cavity before roasting chicken or Cornish game hens, or stuff a fish with the leaves before grilling. Steep leaves in hot milk for 30 minutes before proceeding with your favorite pudding or dessert sauce recipe.

And as tea or to flavor other drinks, lemon verbena has few rivals.

Description

Type Perennial. Zones 9 to 10.
Size Where hardy, 10 feet tall and 8 feet wide. In containers, 2 to 3 feet tall and 18 inches wide.
Flowers Tiny white and purple flowers in loose, open sprays. Early summer.
Leaves Narrow, pointed leaves to 4 inches long and $1/2$ inch wide in whorls of three or four leaves.
Natural Habitat Native to Chile and Argentina.

How to Grow

Light Full sun.
Soil Humus-rich, moist, well-drained.
Propagation Seeds are difficult to germinate, so it's best to buy a plant. Take cuttings in late spring or early summer.
Care Pinch the growing tips out or cut the entire plant back by half in midsummer to encourage branching. Spray spider mites or whiteflies with horticultural soap. In the autumn, cut the plant back by half and bring indoors before the first frost. Place in bright light and keep the soil barely moist. Increase watering in the

After several years of growth, a lemon verbena plant may bloom during the summer with loose, open sprays of tiny white and purple flowers.

Summer Wine Cooler

8 lemon verbena leaves
1 tablespoon sugar
$^1/_4$ cup boiling water
1 750-ml bottle light, dry red wine, such as Beaujolais or Zinfandel
$^1/_3$ cup dry sherry
1 lemon, thinly sliced
$^1/_2$ teaspoon grated nutmeg
1 quart carbonated water, chilled
8 sprigs lemon verbena

In a small bowl, combine lemon verbena, sugar and water. Stir and crush the leaves with a spoon. Let sit for 30 minutes. Remove the leaves and pour the sugar liquid into a large pitcher. Add the red wine, sherry, lemon slices and nutmeg and stir. Let sit for 30 minutes. Just before serving, add the carbonated water. Serve immediately over ice, garnished with sprigs of lemon verbena. Makes eight servings.

spring and mist the stems with water.

In the Landscape Place lemon verbena where it can easily be brushed against, releasing the fresh, lemony scent. Try placing a pot on the outdoor dining table or near a garden bench.

Where lemon verbena is not hardy, grow it in a container filled with a fast-draining potting mix. Feed monthly during the growing season with balanced fertilizer according to the manufacturer's directions.

Culinary Uses

Harvest Gather leaves as needed, preferably by snipping branch tips. Preserve by drying.

In the Kitchen Use the leaves to flavor fish or poultry dishes, rice, grains, hot or iced drinks, marinades, salad dressings, jellies, vinegars, puddings, cakes, cookies, fruit salads or other fruit desserts.

The leaves tend to be tough, so always chop them finely or remove them before serving if used whole.

Other Uses

Include fresh sprigs of lemon verbena in nosegays or bouquets. Add the dried leaves to potpourris. Drink a tea made from the leaves for insomnia or indigestion. Or moisten a cloth with the tea and use it as a compress for puffy eyes.

You can train lemon verbena as a standard and use it in the formal garden.

LOVAGE

Levisticum officinale
Umbelliferae — carrot family

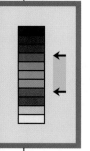

Even as young plants, lovage produces an abundance of celery-flavored leaves that are useful in soups, stews, vinegars or herb blends.

Description
Type Perennial. Zones 4 to 8.
Size 6 feet tall, 2 to 3 feet wide.
Flowers Flat clusters to 4 inches wide of tiny yellow flowers.
Leaves Glossy, bright green, wedge-shaped leaflets with toothed edges on hollow, ribbed stems.
Natural Habitat Native to southern Europe.
Other Species and Cultivars Leaf celery (*Apium graveolens*), also listed as 'Amsterdam Fine Seasoning Celery,' is an annual or biennial that grows to 1 foot tall. It resembles Italian parsley in appearance but the leaves have an intense celery flavor.

How to Grow
Light Full sun to light shade.
Soil Humus-rich, moist, well-drained.
Propagation Sow fresh seed outdoors in late summer or early autumn. Space plants 2 feet apart in the garden, although usually one plant is all you need. Divide in spring or early summer.

For an easy-to-grow celery substitute, nothing beats lovage. The plant is versatile: not only are the leaves a powerful seasoning, but the seeds also bring resonance to pickling mixtures, cheese dips or salad dressings. Plus, you can eat the stems and roots as a vegetable. And there's no better way to drink a Bloody Mary than by sipping it through a hollow lovage stem. The long-lived, bold plants bring a lushness to any garden setting. For those who can't abide freckles, a tea made from the seeds is reputed to fade them away.

Lovage leaves and stems have a celery-like flavor and the stems are hollow rather than solid, making them ideal for sipping tomato juice.

Potato and Lovage Soup

1 pound potatoes, peeled and diced
2 tablespoons butter or margarine
2 tablespoons canola oil
4 cups vegetable stock or broth
1/3 cup minced fresh lovage leaves
1 cup milk
1/2 teaspoon salt
1/4 teaspoon ground black pepper

In a large saucepan, warm the butter and oil over medium-low heat. Add the potatoes and cook, stirring frequently, for 15 minutes. Do not let them brown. Add the stock or broth and lovage, bring to a simmer and cook 20 minutes, or until the potatoes are tender. Pour the soup into a blender and purée. Do this in two batches and hold the lid down tightly. Return the soup to the pan and stir in the milk, salt and pepper. Heat but do not boil. Serve immediately. Makes four servings.

When in bloom, branches of clustered, tiny yellow flowers make lovage as attractive as any ornamental in the garden.

Care Clip off the flower stems; they appear to encourage bushy growth.

In the Landscape Lovage grows big and makes a bold statement in the garden, so plant it near the center of beds or the backs of borders.

Culinary Uses

Harvest Harvest young leaves and stems as needed, since these have the best flavor. Preserve by freezing or drying. Gather the seed heads just as the seeds begin to pop open.

In the Kitchen Add the leaves or stems to green salads, stocks, soups, stews, dried herb blends or vinegars. They also go well with egg or cheese dishes, plus most meats.

Other Uses

Include the leaves and flowers in bouquets. Drink a tea made from the leaves for indigestion, water retention or menstrual pain. Do not take medicinally when pregnant.

Because lovage may grow to 6 feet tall, plant it near the back of a border or toward the center of a bed.

MEXICAN TARRAGON, MEXICAN MARIGOLD MINT

Tagetes lucida
Compositae — daisy family

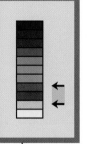

The sunny yellow flowers of Mexican tarragon look great in the garden; the leaves taste great in the kitchen.

A relative of the strongly scented garden marigolds, Mexican marigold has foliage that smells and tastes like candied French tarragon. It is an excellent substitute for the tempermental Gaul, especially in hot, humid climates where French tarragon is difficult to grow. In Mexico, it is used in cooking, such as tucking a leaf into each corn tamale or using them like bay leaves in long-cooked stews or roasts. The ancient Aztec custom is to flavor hot chocolate with a leaf or two. And a few leaves added to the cooking water for corn-on-the-cob or when baking winter squash is sublime. Try them in creamed soups made from winter vegetables like carrots or pumpkin. A tea made from the leaves alleviates indigestion. For ceremonies like baptisms, the fragrant foliage is burned as incense and can also be smoked in pipes or cigarettes.

Description

Type Perennial. Zones 9 to 10.

Size 30 inches tall, 18 inches wide.

Flowers Flat-topped clusters of daisy-like, 1-inch-deep yellow flowers. Late summer and autumn.

Leaves Shiny, narrow, pointed, dark green leaves to 3 inches long and $1/2$ inch wide with toothed edges.

Natural Habitat Southwestern United States, Mexico and Guatemala.

Other species and cultivars Among the other herbal types of marigolds are the signet marigolds, (*T. tenuifolia* 'Lemon Gem', 'Orange Gem' and 'Red Gem') which are annuals growing to 1 foot, with feathery foliage and edible 1-inch single flowers. Irish lace marigold (*T. filfolia*) is a foot-tall annual with edible, anise-scented foliage. Stinking Roger (*T. minuta*), an annual growing to 3 feet tall, repels nematodes and slugs and also prevents weed growth; the dried leaves have an apple-like scent and are used in cooking.

The deep yellow to orange flowers of Mexican tarragon are edible, but it is the tarragon-flavored foliage that bring the most flavor to foods.

Mexican marigold grows well in a container filled with a fast-draining potting mix. Feed monthly during the growing season with balanced fertilizer according to the manufacturer's directions. If desired, bring it indoors during the winter, placing it in bright light.

Culinary Uses

Harvest Gather the leaves as needed. Preserve by drying.

In the Kitchen Substitute Mexican tarragon in any dish where French tarragon is used, such as in salads, sauces, butters, vinegars or with vegetables, poultry or fish. Don't add as much, however, as the flavor is much more pronounced. Mexican tarragon withstands longer cooking than the French version.

Other Uses

Toss dried stems on the grill or bonfire to repel insects. Drink a tea made from the leaves for indigestion or hiccups. Washing skin with the tea is said to remove ticks.

How to Grow

Light Full sun.

Soil Humus-rich, moist, well-drained.

Propagation Sow seeds indoors six weeks before the last frost in spring. Transplant to the garden after all frost danger is past. Space plants 1 foot apart. Propagate by division or cuttings in spring.

Care Where it isn't hardy, Mexican marigold is treated as an annual or brought indoors during the winter. In climates with a long growing season, cut the plants back after flowering for fresh, new foliage.

In the Landscape Although Mexican marigold doesn't begin blooming until late summer, the plants are handsome and versatile enough for anywhere in the garden.

Native to southwestern United States, Mexico and Guatemala, Mexican tarragon survives hot summer days much better than French tarragon.

Summer Squash and Mexican Tarragon Fritters

2 cups grated summer squash
1/2 cup finely minced scallions
1 tablespoon minced fresh Mexican tarragon
1/3 cup unbleached all-purpose flour
1/2 teaspoon salt
1/4 teaspoon ground black pepper
1 large egg
1/4 cup water
2 tablespoons canola oil

In a large bowl, combine squash, scallions, Mexican tarragon, flour, salt and pepper. In a small bowl, whisk the egg and water together. Stir into the squash mixture. Warm the oil in a non-stick skillet over medium heat. Drop scant quarter-cups of the squash mixture into the skillet. Flatten each one out with a spatula and cook until golden brown on the bottom. Flip over and cook until golden brown on the other side. Serve immediately. Makes four servings.

MINT

Mentha species and cultivars
Labiatae — mint family

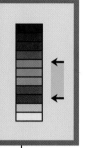

Spearmint is the favorite of all the mints for cooking. Its flavor adapts to desserts as well as to main courses, salads and grains.

Mint, with its cool, bracing scent and flavor, is appreciated in cuisines around the world, from England to the Mediterranean and Middle East, India, Southeast Asia, Mexico and the United States. It is particularly associated with the American South because of the ubiquity of mint in iced tea, to say nothing of mint juleps. But to speak of mint in the singular is somewhat erroneous, for to say that there is a maze of mint is an understatement. There is somewhere between one-and-a-half to two-dozen species, plus hundreds of varieties. This is because mints so readily hybridize, both in nature and in cultivation. Often the same or very similar ones are given different names. Be willing to explore and experiment.

Basically, mints are divided into two camps, peppermint (*M.* x *piperita*) and spearmint (*M. spicata*). The menthol in the peppermint group causes an anesthetic action that elicits a cooling sensation on the palate. Mints in this group are most often used in desserts. The spearmint group does not contain menthol, and its members are more adaptable to a wide range of cooking. There are no hard-and-fast rules to using them, however, as it really comes down to a matter of personal taste.

Description

Type Perennial. Zones 3 to 9.

Size Most culinary types grow to 2 feet tall, but there are some low-growing ornamental ones. Indefinite spread.

Flowers Whorled spikes of tiny lavender, pink or white flowers. Summer.

Leaves Oval, pointed, toothed leaves generally 1 to 3 inches long. Several have smaller leaves to $^1/_2$ inch long.

'Kentucky Colonel' mint shows off large, wrinkled leaves and offers an intensely "spearmint" flavor and scent.

Natural Habitat Most are native to Europe and Asia, but some are from North America, Africa or Australia.

Other Species and Cultivars Besides "regular" peppermint, try some of the varieties such as 'Blackstem', 'Blue Balsam' and 'Candy Mint'. Other mints with a peppermint flavor include Japanese mint (*M. arvensis* var. *piperascens*), American mint (*M. arvensis* var. *villosa*), horsemint (*M. longifolia*), curly peppermint (*M. aquatica* 'Crispa') and variegated peppermint (*M. x piperata* 'Variegata').

Among the spearmint clan are Austrian mint (*M. x gracilis*) along with its variegated, golden and Vietnamese forms: Bowles' mint (*M. x villosa* var. *alopecuroides*), Chinese mint (*M. haplocalyx*), curly spearmint (*M. x smithiana* 'Crispa'), Kentucky Colonel mint (*M. x cordifolia*), 'Mint-the-Best' (*M. x spicata* 'Mint-the-Best') and Moroccan mint (*M. x spicata* 'Moroccan').

Then there is the wide array of mints with some other flavor intermingled with the minty characteristics. These include apple mint (*M. suaveloens*), orange mint (*M. x piperita* 'Citrata'), chocolate mint (*M. x piperata* 'Mitcham'), grapefruit mint (*M. 'Grapefruit'*), Hillary's sweet lemon mint (*M. 'Hillary's Sweet Lemon'*) and pineapple mint (*M. suaveolens* 'Variegata').

For those who can't make up their minds, try doublemint (*M. 'Doublemint'*), which is a variety that contains both spearmint and peppermint oils. It is particularly appropriate when cooking Southeast Asian dishes.

Pennyroyal (*M. pulegium*) and Australian pennyroyal (*M. satureioides*) were once widely used in home reme-

Besides the distinctive fragrance, peppermint also often has purplish-red stems. All mints and their relatives have square stems.

Apple mint has a fruity, spearmint scent and flavor. The rounded, wrinkly leaves are usually slightly downy.

dies, but research has shown that these should not be taken internally. Still, many people enjoy growing them for their pungent scent.

For those who garden in Zones 7 to 9, choose a moist, shady place for Corsican mint (*M. requienii*). Growing almost flat on the ground, with tiny $^3/_8$-inch leaves, its fragance is such that some people call it the creme de menthe plant.

If that isn't enough mint for you, there are the mint imposters. These include: Korean mint (*Agastache rugosa*), growing to 5 feet tall in Zones 6 to 9; the mountain mint clan (*Pycnanthemum flexuosum, P. incanum, P. pilosum,* and *P. virginianum*), all North American natives growing to 3 feet tall in Zones 5 to 10; and Jamaican mint (*Micromeria viminea*), growing to 12 inches tall with tiny leaves in Zones

Mint plants spread and grow abundantly, yielding large quantities of leaves for drying to use in cooking and potpourri.

7 to 10 or used as a house-plant.

How to Grow
Light Light shade, but full sun is tolerated.

Soil Humus-rich, moist, well-drained.

Propagation Few mints come true from seed. It's better to buy plants. Space plants 18 to 24 inches apart. Divide or take cuttings in spring or autumn.

Care To contain a plant, sink a barrier 12 inches into the soil on all sides or cut the bottom out of a 5-gallon bucket and

Moroccan Pilaf

2 tablespoons canola oil
$^1/_2$ cup finely chopped onion
2 cloves garlic, minced
$^1/_2$ teaspoon ground cardamom
$^1/_2$ teaspoon ground cinnamon
$^1/_2$ teaspoon ground cloves
$^1/_2$ teaspoon ground black pepper
1 cup brown rice
2 cups water
1 cup peeled, seeded and diced tomato
$^1/_2$ cup fresh or frozen peas
$^1/_2$ cup grated carrots
$^1/_2$ cup slivered, toasted almonds
$^1/_4$ cup currants
2 tablespoons lemon juice
1 teaspoon salt
$^1/_2$ cup minced fresh spearmint leaves

In a large saucepan, warm the oil over medium-high heat, then add the onion and garlic. Cook, stirring, for about 3 minutes or until soft. Add the cardamom, cinnamon, cloves and rice. Continue to cook, stirring, for 2 minutes. Stir in the water, tomatoes, peas, carrots, almonds, currants, lemon juice and salt. Bring to a boil, reduce heat to low, cover and cook about 50 minutes or until the rice is tender. Stir in the mint, cover and let stand for 5 minutes before serving. Makes six servings.

Mint's rapidly spreading underground runners mean that a large area of the garden will soon be filled with delicious and soothing scents.

Pineapple mint, a variegated version of apple mint, produces handsome, white-edged leaves and a sweet pineapple fragrance.

Lime-Mint Smoothie

1 cup non-fat vanilla frozen yogurt
3/4 cup non-fat milk
1/4 cup frozen limeade concentrate
1/4 cup fresh peppermint leaves

Combine frozen yogurt, milk, limeade concentrate and mint in a blender and blend until smooth. Serve immediately. Makes two servings.

bury it to within an inch of the rim. Spray aphids, spider mites or flea beetles with horticultural soap. Remove and destroy mints that develop fungal diseases such as rust.

In the Landscape When you restrain mint's roots, they are perfectly acceptable members of the herb garden or flower border. Try to choose an area that gets some shade. Only if you have a wild corner of the yard or an area that can easily be mowed around should you plant without any boundaries.

One of the best ways to confine the mints: grow them in containers. Fill containers with a fast-draining potting mix and give a monthly feeding during the growing season with balanced fertilizer according to the manufacturer's directions. If desired, bring mints indoors during the winter, placing them in bright light. Or leave the pots outdoors in a protected place, and make sure the plants are mulched.

Culinary Uses

Harvest Gather the leaves as needed. Preserve by drying. Pick the flowers as they open.

In the Kitchen

Use mint in drinks, butters, vinegars, jellies, sauces, relishes, soups, ice creams, sorbets, cookies, fruit salads or desserts. Crystallize the leaves. Mint goes well with carrots, cucumbers, eggplant, peas, potatoes, tomatoes, yogurt dips and lamb. Wait to chop mint until just before adding to a dish, as it quickly blackens and loses flavor.

Other Uses

Include stems of mint as foliage in bouquets. Include the dried leaves in potpourris. Drink a tea made from mint for indigestion, hiccups, insomnia, colds or flu. You can also add the tea to bath water, use it as a hair rinse or facial tonic, or apply it to chapped skin.

Orange mint is sometimes labeled bergamot mint because the citrus scent and flavor resembles bergamot oranges.

NASTURTIUM

Tropaeolum majus
Tropaeolaceae — nasturtium family

Indian cress is another common name for nasturtiums, which is quite appropriate, as these spicy-flavored leaves have notes of East Indian spices combined with the taste of peppery watercress. Resembling miniature lily pads, the leaves (whole or minced) give green salads a satisfying bite. The edible flowers mimic the leaves but with a milder flavor. "Yellow-lark's-heels" is the rather poetic name that 17th-century herbalist John Parkinson called the nasturtium. He would be surprised at the variety of colors that 20th-century gardeners can select from, including scarlet, orange, mahogany, cherry-rose, gold, cream, salmon, tangerine and peach. These multiple colors bring out the

artist in the cooking gardener. A confetti of finely chopped flowers of different shades makes a pretty herb butter for bread or for melting over vegetables, pasta or grilled salmon. A vinegar made from the leaves or flowers belongs on the pantry shelf, and also makes a unique gift for other gardeners or cooks.

Description

Type Annual.
Size Bush types to 1 foot; vining type to 6 feet.
Flowers Funnel-shaped and spurred flowers, $1^1/2$ to 2 inches across, with five petals, in shades of red, orange and yellow. Summer through autumn.
Leaves Round, 2 to 7 inches across, with wavy margins.
Natural Habitat Native to South America.
Other Species and Cultivars
'Alaska' has cream-and-green mottled foliage and single flowers on mounding, 10-inch plants. It is a chef's favorite as a garnish, not only for its beauty

Nasturtium flowers add a colorful touch to soups or salads.

but also for its exceptional taste. The 'Whirlybird' series has upward-facing, double flowers held well above the foliage of the mounding, 12-inch plants. 'Peach Melba' forms 10-inch mounds with single flowers, the color of a white peach with a throat of raspberry red, held above the leaves. Along this same line are 'Butter Cream' with semi-double, pale yellow flowers, and 'Creamsicle' with single flowers in a swirl of pale orange and creamy white centered with a crimson throat. 'Jewel Mix' is an old-fashioned blend of

'Whirlybird' nasturtiums are favored for their compact growth and large, upward-facing flowers held well above the leaves.

Old-fashioned 'Glorious Gleam' nasturtiums feature trailing stems that are ideal for tumbling over a wall or climbing up fences and trellises.

TIP Unripe nasturtium seedpods easily make acceptable substitutes for capers. Pick the seedpods when they are still green and $1/4$ inch in diameter. Place in a heat-proof glass jar and pour heated vinegar over them. Cap with a nonreactive lid and store in the refrigerator. Wait one week before using.

Nasturtium Roll-Ups

$1/2$ cup homemade yogurt cheese or whipped low-fat cream cheese
2 tablespoons minced fresh nasturtium flowers
2 tablespoons minced walnuts
1 tablespoon minced fresh chives
16 large nasturtium leaves, washed and dried
16 nasturtium flowers with stems

In a small bowl, combine cheese, flowers and nuts. Spread a mounded teaspoon of the mixture on a leaf. Roll the leaf around the filling and tie with the stem of the nasturtium flower. The flower should rest on the rolled leaf. Trim the stem to 1 inch. Serve immediately or cover and chill. Makes about twenty-four.

brightly colored, single flowers on mounding plants.

'Empress of India' is a particularly handsome heirloom variety with vermilion-red flowers on cascading mounds of blue-green leaves. Trailing even more are the 6- to 8-foot stems of 'Glorious Gleam', which produces large, fragrant, single and semi-double flowers.

How to Grow
Light Full sun.
Soil Humus-rich, moist, well-drained.
Propagation Sow seed indoors four weeks before the last spring frost, transplanting to the garden when all danger of frost is past. Or, sow directly outdoors after the last spring frost. Plant seeds $1/2$ inch deep. Space plants 6 to 10 inches apart.

'Alaska' is a nasturtium with variegated cream-and-green leaves on low-growing, compact plants.

Nasturtiums prefer poor soils over nice, fertile types.

Care If your plants' leaves are very large or if there aren't many blooms, then the soil is too fertile. Control aphids with a forceful spray of water from the garden hose or spray with horticultural soap. In areas with hot summers, nasturtiums sometimes grow better in light shade. In mild-winter areas, nasturtiums self-sow.
In the Landscape The low, mounding forms of nasturtiums make bright, continuously blooming additions to flower beds and borders or the kitchen or herb garden. Plant them in masses or as an edging. Allow the trailing types to cover an area of ground, or train them to climb a fence, trellis or wall.

Nasturtiums grow well in containers with a fast-draining potting mix. Feed monthly during the growing season with balanced fertilizer according to the manufacturer's directions.

Culinary Uses
Harvest Gather the leaves at any time as needed. Pick flowers just as they open. Cut the leaves and flowers with the stems attached.
In the Kitchen Add the leaves or flowers to salads, butters, vinegars, dips, cheese spreads, egg dishes or finger sandwiches. Use as a garnish.

Other Uses
Drink a tea made from the leaves for water retention or to improve skin and hair. Externally, the tea has antiseptic properties.

'Empress of India' is an heirloom nasturtium with vermilion-red flowers set off by masses of deep blue-green leaves; it grows in cascading mounds.

OREGANO

Origanum species and cultivars
Labiatae — mint family

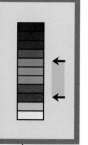

Oregano comes from a large family—there are some 20 members in the genus.

leaved oregano (*O. microphyllum*), Syrian oregano (*O. maru*) and Turkestan oregano (variously listed as *O. turkistanica* or *O. tyttanicum*).

Description

Type Perennial. Zones 5 to 9.
Size 18 inches to 2 feet tall, 18 inches wide.

Although the genus name is derived from ancient Greek words meaning joy-of-the-mountain, trying to find one with that true oregano flavor can be anything but fun. Sorting out the naming has frustrated botanists, gardeners and cooks for years. Common oregano (*O. vulgare*), also called wild marjoram, often has very little flavor. You'll usually be more successful with the Greek oregano that is botanically *O. vulgare* 'Hirtum' but may also be labelled *O. heracleoticum*. Pot marjoram (*O. onites*) is also called Greek oregano, but it usually has little flavor. Other good culinary oreganos include Kaliteri oregano (*O. 'Kaliteri'*), small-

'Compacta', a form of oregano, has ground-hugging growth and stiff, upright stems with small leaves and clusters of pink flowers.

Flowers Clusters of $1/4$-inch, rose-purple to white flowers. Summer to autumn.
Leaves Oval, pointed, bright green leaves $1/2$- to 2-inches long.
Natural Habitat Native to the Mediterranean region west to central Asia.
Other Species and Cultivars There is another plant called Mexican oregano (*Lippia graveolens*) that is an oregano taste-alike but unrelated to each other or to *Origanum*. Lippia is native to tropical Africa and Latin America and is a 6-foot shrub with rough-textured leaves that resemble those of the related lantana. Cuban oregano (*Plectranthus amboinicus*) is another unrelated plant with an oregano flavor. It is a sprawling plant growing to 2 feet tall with succulent stems and leaves. Both of these are hardy in Zones 9 and 10.

Many members of the *Origanum* genus are beautiful ornamental plants, but the leaves have no flavor.

How to Grow

Light Full sun, except for golden forms, which do best in light shade.

Dwarf oregano has a nice, compact habit, making it great for containers.

Because common oregano, also known as wild marjoram, is so variable from seed, gently rub a leaf before buying to make sure it has a good aroma.

Soil Well-drained.
Propagation Because the flavor varies greatly from seed-started plants, it's better to purchase plants that are propagated by cuttings or division from plants known

Because of all the confusion with plants that taste like oregano, herb researchers have begun to call oregano a flavor as opposed to calling it a single genus or species.

to have good flavor. Take cuttings in summer or divide in spring or autumn. Space plants 18 inches apart.
Care Spray spider mites with horticultural soap. In Zone 5, protect plants with a winter mulch.
In the Landscape The true oreganos (*Origanum*) generally form rounded, bushy, spreading plants that make good groundcover or filler plants in the garden.

You can also grow oreganos in containers filled with fast-draining potting mix. Feed monthly with a balanced fertilizer according to the manufacturer's directions.

Culinary Uses

Harvest Gather the leaves as needed. For drying, cut plants back to 3 inches just before flowering. With a long growing season, a second harvest is possible. Preserve by drying or freezing.
In the Kitchen Yes, place the leaves in tomato sauce

Oregano plants also make great ornamentals.

for pasta or pizza, but also include them in salads, butters, vinegars or marinades. Plus, the flavor complements cheese and egg dishes, beef, pork, poultry, game, beans, eggplant and summer squash.

Other Uses

Use the stems and flowers in bouquets or nosegays. The dried flowers are also useful in crafts. Make a tea from the leaves for indigestion, headaches or coughs. Add the tea to bathwater for relief of aching muscles or joints.

Even if you end up with an oregano that does not have much flavor, you can still enjoy the plants for their summer- and autumn-blooming flowers.

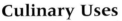

Marinated Olives

6 ounces black or green olives (or a mixture), drained
1/4 cup fresh oregano leaves
1/2 teaspoon whole black peppercorns
3 cloves garlic, peeled
1/2 teaspoon lemon zest
1 bay leaf
1 cup lemon juice or herb-flavored vinegar, or a combination

In a pint glass jar, layer olives with the oregano, peppercorns, garlic, lemon zest and bay. Pour in the lemon juice or vinegar, adding more to cover, if necessary. Cover with a piece of plastic wrap, then the screw-on lid. Store in the refrigerator, waiting several days before serving to allow flavors to blend. Makes 6 ounces.

PARSLEY

Petroselinum crispum
Umbelliferae — carrot family

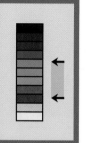

The truest remark that can be made about both curly and Italian parsleys is that gardeners who enjoy cooking simply cannot be without them. Both types bring out the flavor of other herbs and combine especially well with marjoram, oregano, rosemary and thyme. Parsley is one of the richest sources of vitamin C. It also contains vitamin A, several B vitamins, calcium and iron, plus it reduces allergies and is an effective antioxidant. And that garnish on the edge of your plate? Don't push it away, but eat it instead to freshen your breath.

Although curly parsley (*P. crispum* 'Moss Curled', also called *P. c.* var. *crispum*) is favored for its garnishing qualities and ease in chopping, for the best flavor, choose the flat-leaf, Italian form (*P. crispum* 'Italian', also called *P. c.* var. *neopolitanum*).

Description
Type Biennial, often grown as an annual. Zones 5 to 9.
Size 8 to 18 inches tall.
Flowers Flat clusters of tiny, greenish-yellow flowers. Late fall or early spring of the following year.
Leaves Finely divided into many sections, either flat like celery or curled and frilly.

Curly parsley, with its bright green, frilly leaves, adds beauty to a planting of annual flowers.

Natural Habitat Native from Lebanon to Sardinia.
Other Species and Cultivars
There are a number of improved strains of curly parsley, including 'Green River' (which is especially bushy, cold and heat tolerant, and disease resistant) and 'Frisca' (a Dutch variety with a sweet, clean flavor). 'Gigante d'Italia' is an heirloom Italian type with a rich, mellow, sweet flavor. Hamburg parsley (*P. crispum* var. *tuberosum*) is grown for its thick, fleshy, edible taproot that is eaten raw in salads or cooked as a vegetable. The leaves are also edible.

The Japanese herb called mitsuba, or wild chervil (*Cryptotaenia canadensis*), has a flavor somewhere between parsley and celery. It is a perennial that grows to 3 feet tall and 2 feet wide in shady conditions in Zones 4 to 9 and readily self-sows.

How to Grow
Light Full sun to light shade.
Soil Humus-rich, moist, well-drained.

For flavor in the kitchen, flat-leaf, or Italian, parsley is the best.

In ancient Greek gardens, vivid green parsley was thickly planted with the blue-green of rue as a striking scheme for the edging of garden beds. The combination of the two herbs is the derivation of a curious aphorism. If one is "at the parsley and the rue," it denotes that the person is on the cutting edge of a particular situation.

Curly parsley readily grows in a container, but be sure to fertilize monthly so that the plant produces abundant foliage all summer long.

Propagation Seed is very slow to germinate. To speed up the process, soak overnight in warm water then rinse thoroughly before planting. Sow indoors 8 weeks before the last spring frost. Transplant outdoors one week before the last frost. Space plants 8 to 12 inches apart, being careful not to damage the tap root. If allowed to go to seed, parsley self-sows.

Care Parsley is a favorite food of swallowtail butterfly caterpillars. Grow enough for both you and them. To prolong the life of parsley for at least a couple of weeks, cut out the flower stalks as they appear.

In the Landscape Curly parsley is an excellent edging plant for beds and borders in flower, herb or kitchen gardens. Italian parsley is an attractive foliage plant.

Parsley grows well in containers with a fast-draining potting mix. Feed monthly during the growing season with balanced fertilizer according to the manufacturer's directions. Start seeds or buy young plants in the fall to pot up for growing indoors with bright light in winter. Or, grow parsley during the winter in a coldframe.

Culinary Uses

Harvest Gather the leaves whenever you need them. Cut off the stems at the base on the outside of the plant. Remove the stems before using as they tend to be bitter. Preserve by drying or freezing.

In the Kitchen Use parsley leaves in just about any food except dessert. Of special note is its use in Middle Eastern tabbouleh (a salad of bulgur, tomatoes, onion, parsley, mint and olive oil), the French persillade (a mixture of finely chopped parsley and garlic added as a flavoring just before cooking is completed), and the bouquet garni (a cluster of parsley, thyme and bay leaf for flavoring soups, stews and broths).

Other Uses

Curly parsley make a pretty addition to nosegays. Drink a tea made from parsley leaves to relieve water retention or indigestion, or as a mild laxative. Moisten a cloth with the tea and place on sprains, sores or insect bites. Also use parsley as a facial tonic or hair rinse, or add it to bathwater.

Green Sauce

1 slice white or whole-wheat bread, crusts removed
1/4 cup extra-virgin olive oil
1 cup fresh parsley
1 tablespoon capers
2 cloves garlic, minced
1 anchovy fillet or small piece of seaweed soaked in water
1 tablespoon lemon juice

Tear the bread into small pieces and put in a small bowl. Pour in the oil. Let it soak for 15 minutes. In a food processor, combine parsley, capers, garlic, anchovy or seaweed, lemon juice and the bread-oil mixture. Process until smooth. Serve as a sauce over steamed or grilled vegetables, rice, grilled fish or grilled chicken. Makes four servings.

PINKS

Dianthus species and cultivars
Caryophyllaceae — carnation family

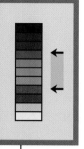

Producing abundant masses of ground-hugging gray-green leaves, pinks bear clove-scented flowers in spring.

Pinks belong to the genus *Dianthus*, or the "divine flower" as it was named in ancient times. The Greeks and Romans grew pinks for the food and medicinal values of these charming, clove-scented flowers. Today, pinks may be more often thought of for their charm in the garden, but don't overlook what they can bring to breakfast as a syrup for pancakes, to lunch as a dessert sorbet, to afternoon tea as a jelly for scones, to a dinner salad in the vinaigrette or to late evening in a cordial. And this is just the beginning of ways to use the flowers in cooking. In the garden, pinks are simpler versions of the florist carnation. Low spreading mounds of gray-green foliage are covered from spring into summer with delicate flowers in shades of pink, red or white.

Description

Type Perennial or biennial. Hardiness varies with the species.

Size 8 to 20 inches tall, 8 to 24 inches wide.

Flowers Five or more frilly, fringed or toothed petals, either solid or with a contrasting eye, in shades of pink, red and white.

Leaves Evergreen, gray-green, grassy leaves to 2 inches long and 1/4 inch wide.

Natural Habitat
Mediterranean, Balkans and Asia Minor.

Other Species and Cultivars
Hundreds of species and cultivars of pinks exist. For the garden and cooking, concentrate on the Cheddar pink (*D. gratianopolitanus*), cottage pink (*D. plumarius*) and the lilac pink (*D. superbus*).

Cheddar pinks are named after the Cheddar Gorge in Somerset, England. They grow 8 to 12 inches tall and 12 to 18 inches wide, forming a dense mat of blue-gray leaves. The pink, fringed, strongly fragrant, 3/4-inch flowers bloom in spring and early summer, one or two to a stem. Cultivars include 'Bath's Pink', a fringed, soft pink and 'Karlik', a fringed, deep pink. Perennial, hardy in Zones 5 to 8.

Cottage pinks, also known as grass or Scotch pinks, grow to 12 inches tall in a loose mound to 12 inches wide with gray, 4-inch leaves. The 1- to 1½-inch flowers are borne on 10-inch stems in clusters of 2 to 5 spicily fragrant flowers (single, double or semidouble). Plants bloom for a long period if the faded flower stems are cut back to the ground. Crosses between the cottage pink and the clove pink (*D. caryophyllus*) have produced the modern garden pinks most often grown today. Two of the most popular and fragrant ones are 'Helen', with double pink flowers, and 'Doris', with semidouble pink flowers and a darker eye. Perennial, hardy in Zones 4 to 8.

Lilac pinks grow 1 to 2 feet tall and 18 inches wide, forming mounds of green, 2-inch leaves. The plants continuously produce flowering stems bearing 2 to 12, intensely fragrant, 2-inch flowers with deeply fringed petals in shades of pale lilac to rose purple. 'Rainbow Loveliness' is an heirloom strain you can start from seed; the flowers may be pink, red or purple. Biennial, hardy in Zones 4 to 8.

Pinks go well with anything fruity or sweet.

> ## Pink Sauce
>
> 2 cups fresh or frozen and thawed strawberries (unsweetened)
> ¼ cup fresh dianthus (pinks) petals, white heel removed
> 2 tablespoons confectioners' sugar
> 1 tablespoon lemon juice
>
> If necessary, hull the strawberries. Place berries, pinks, sugar and lemon juice in a food processor. Process until smooth. Place in an airtight container and refrigerate. Serve over angel food or pound cake, waffles or vanilla mousse, preferably with fresh, sliced strawberries and crystallized dianthus petals. Makes six servings.

How to Grow

Light Full sun.

Soil Humus-rich, moist, well-drained; grows best with neutral to alkaline soil. Well-drained soil in winter is of the utmost importance.

Propagation Sow seed indoors four to six weeks before the last spring frost and plant out after all frost danger is past. Space plants 1 foot apart. You may not be able to propagate named varieties from seed. Divide in summer after flowering. Take cuttings in spring. Layer in late summer.

Care After flowering, cut off the stems of faded flowers and trim back to shape or maintain size. Perennial pinks may need dividing after about three years to maintain vigor. Spray spider mites with horticultural soap.

In the Landscape Pinks have been planted anywhere from the largest formal garden to the most casual cottage garden. They soften the edges of the garden, whether tumbling over a wall or stretching from a border into a pathway. For the ultimate in fragrance and charm, plant them with old-fashioned roses.

Pinks grow well in containers with a fast-draining potting mix. Feed monthly during the growing season with balanced fertilizer according to the manufacturer's directions. Place the pots in a protected location and cover with mulch during the winter.

Culinary Uses

Harvest Pick the flowers just as they open. Remove the stems back almost to the ground. Pull the petals loose and cut off the narrow, white, bitter base before using. Preserve by drying.

In the Kitchen Use pinks to flavor white wine, liqueurs, sugar syrups, vinegars, butters, cream cheese, cookies, cakes, jellies, sorbets, ice creams or teas. Add the fresh petals to salads or fruit dishes. Crystallize the petals for decorating pastries.

Other Uses

Pinks are great in bouquets or nosegays. Add the dried flowers to potpourris.

The flowers of pinks bring a sweet clove taste to drinks, desserts, jellies, fruit salads and cream cheese.

ROSE

Rosa species and cultivars
Rosaceae - rose family

For over 3,000 years, roses have been considered the queen of flowers, and the folklore surrounding them fills volumes. One of the most beloved of fragrances, rose oil, finds its way into all manner of perfumes and toiletries. At home, the scent is best captured in potpourris. The astringent petals have played a role in medicines since the times of the ancient Greeks, Romans, Persians and Chinese, especially for sore throats and stomach ailments. The tart fruits, called hips, are a rich source of vitamin C, plus they contain vitamins A, B and E. In the kitchen, rose hips have a wide range of uses similar to other berry fruit. Fragrant petals find their way into pastries or fruit desserts.

Description

Type Deciduous or evergreen woody shrub. Hardiness varies.

Size 1 to 25 feet tall, 1 to 10 feet across.

Flowers Clusters of 5- to many-petaled flowers, 1 to 5 inches across, in shades of pink, magenta, rose, red, yellow and white.

Leaves Oval, pointed leaflets 1 to 2 inches long.

Natural Habitat Middle East, Asia and North America.

Other Species and Cultivars With about 200 species and over 10,000 cultivars of roses, the hardest part of growing

Before using rose petals for flavoring food, cut off the bitter white base.

them may be choosing which roses to grow. For the herb garden, many people look first to the apothecary rose (*R. gallica* var. *officinalis*), growing to 3 feet tall and as wide, although it will spread further with time. It blooms once in early summer with 3-inch, deep pink flowers followed by brick-red hips. 'The Herbalist', a David Austin English rose, is very similar but repeat-blooms. Some of the other groups of old roses with fragrant flowers include the Alba, Bourbon, Centifolia, Damask and Moss roses. But you can cook with any fragrant rose, new or old, that has not been treated with pesticides. Some of the best producers of hips are the apple

rose (*R. pomifera*), dog rose (*R. canina*), eglantine rose (*R. eglanteria*) and the rugosa rose (*R. rugosa*).

How to Grow

Light Full sun.
Soil Humus-rich, moist, well-drained.

When using fragrant rose petals in cooking, be sure that the plants have not been sprayed with a pesticide that is not formulated for edibles.

Recognize Rugosa roses by their rough-textured leaves. Besides the clove-scented flowers, these roses also produce an abundance of hips.

Rose Petal Pudding

1 12.3-ounce package lite silken firm tofu
⅔ cup sugar
½ cup fresh rose petals, white heel removed
2 teaspoons rose water or vanilla
Pinch of salt

Crumble the tofu into a food processor. Add the sugar, petals, rose water or vanilla, and salt. Process until creamy and thick. Put into an airtight container and chill for at least 30 minutes. Spoon into dessert dishes and decorate with fresh or crystallized rose petals. Makes four servings.

Propagation Cuttings taken in spring or fall.

Care Space 1 to 8 feet apart, depending on mature size. For easiest maintenance, choose a variety that is well-suited to both the heat and cold of your region. For most roses, cut off faded flowers and prune plants from spring until late summer to maintain size and shape. If growing roses for hips, do not prune off the flowers. Control insect pests with horticultural soap or pyrethrum. Control fungus diseases with a commercial baking soda spray.

In the Landscape From the daintiest miniatures growing only a foot tall in containers to climbing types reaching 25 feet up a wall or along a fence, roses can be a spectacular element in any part of the sunny garden.

Rose varieties that grow from 1 to 3 feet tall do well in containers with a fast-draining potting mix and a monthly feeding during the growing season with balanced fertilizer according to the manufacturer's directions. Overwinter in a protected place, covering the pot and plant with mulch.

Rose petals are pretty, and you can also crystallize them in desserts.

Culinary Uses

Harvest Pick the flowers just as they open. Pull the petals loose and cut off the bitter white base if using in food. Preserve by drying. Pick the hips as they ripen. Cut in half and remove the fuzzy seeds. Preserve by freezing or drying.

In the Kitchen Use the petals to flavor butters, vinegars, sugar, sugar syrups, jellies, cream cheese, fruit desserts, cookies, cakes, sorbets or ice creams. Crystallize the petals for decorating pastries. Use the hips in syrups, jellies, jams, teas, fruit soups, pies, quick breads or muffins.

Other Uses

Roses are without peer as a cut flower in bouquets or as the centerpiece in a nosegay. Use the dried petals in potpourri. Drink a tea made from the hips for a sore throat, cold or indigestion. Use a tea from the petals as a facial tonic or added to bathwater.

Take time to sit down and enjoy roses' beauty and fragrance.

ROSEMARY

Rosmarinus officinalis
Labiatae — mint family

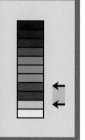

Rosemary's edible blooms vary from dark blue to pale blue, pink and white, depending on the cultivar.

Rosemary is among the most familiar of herbs. Even if you never cook with rosemary, it is a must-have for the garden, just to be able to brush it to release the refreshing, resinous fragrance. One whiff of the scent of rosemary evokes "a beaker full of the warm south," wrote English poet John Keats, referring to the Mediterranean region where rosemary is native. Rosemary has long been cultivated throughout Europe and is surrounded by folklore. Often associated with memory, rosemary was worn in garlands by ancient Greek students studying for exams and memorialized by Ophelia in Shakespeare's *Hamlet* with, "There's rosemary, that's for remembrance." In the kitchen, remember how versatile rosemary can be with its piney yet sweet, vaguely mint and ginger flavor.

Description
Type Evergreen, woody perennial. Zones 8 to 10.
Size 2 to 6 feet tall, 1 to 4 feet wide.
Flowers Pale blue, $1/2$-inch, edible flowers in clusters of two or three, along the branches. Late winter to early spring.
Leaves Needle-like, to $1^{1}/2$ inches long and $1/8$ inch wide.
Natural Habitat Native to Mediterranean, Portugal and northwestern Spain.

Other Species and Cultivars
There are over three dozen cultivars of rosemary. Some variations are in the size, shape or color of the leaf, including variegated and golden forms. There are also cultivars with a stronger than normal pine scent. Other types may have dark blue, pink or white flowers; especially noteworthy is 'Majorca Pink', which blooms for a long period. Some cultivars have cascading growth, while other are stiffly upright. 'Arp', 'Salem' and 'Hill Hardy' are said to withstand winter temperatures to Zone 5.

How to Grow
Light Full sun.
Soil Well-drained.
Propagation Seed is difficult to germinate; plants are very slow to develop and not robust. It is better to take cuttings or layer in late summer. Space plants 1 to 3 feet apart, planting outdoors when night temperatures are consistently 55°F or warmer.
Care Pinch out the growing tips on rosemary to encourage

Cascading or creeping types of rosemary look magnificent tumbling along walls or spilling over the edges of containers.

You can grow rosemary year-round in a container. Feed monthly during the growing season with a balanced fertilizer.

Onion, Tomato and Rosemary Tart

2 tablespoons extra-virgin olive oil
1 large onion, thinly sliced
1 clove garlic, minced
2 cups peeled, seeded and chopped tomatoes
2 teaspoons minced fresh rosemary leaves
1/2 teaspoon salt
1/4 teaspoon freshly ground black pepper
1 cup shredded mozzarella cheese
1/2 cup grated Parmesan cheese
1 12-ounce pre-baked pizza crust

Preheat oven to 450°F. In a large non-stick skillet, warm the oil over medium heat. Stir in the onions and garlic then cook, stirring occasionally, until soft. Add tomatoes, rosemary, salt and pepper. Reduce heat to low, cover, and simmer for 5 minutes. Remove lid and cook an additional 5 minutes, stirring occasionally. Lightly brush pizza crust with olive oil. Sprinkle 1/2 cup of the mozzarella and all the Parmesan cheese over the pizza crust. Spread on the tomato mixture and sprinkle with the remaining 1/2 cup mozzarella. Put in the oven and reduce heat to 425°F. Bake for 10 minutes. Makes six servings.

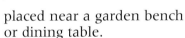

In warmer climates or when successfully overwintered indoors, rosemary grows into a woody shrub to 6 feet tall.

bushy growth. You can train plants into topiary standards. Control aphids, mealybugs, spider mites or whiteflies with horticultural soap.

In the Landscape Where rosemary is hardy, it can develop into large, spectacular plants in the garden. The creeping types are especially effective tumbling over walls. In colder climates, even the extra-hardy types seldom attain such dimensions. Still, a well-grown plant in a container can make a splendid statement, either as a focal point in the garden or placed near a garden bench or dining table.

Rosemary readily grows in containers filled with fast-draining potting mix and a monthly feeding with a balanced fertilizer according to the manufacturer's directions. In climates colder than Zone 8, bring the pots indoors in winter, placing in bright light. Watering container-grown rosemary in winter is a juggling act between too much and not enough. There is no surefire method of success.

Culinary Uses

Harvest Gather leaves as needed. Preserve by drying. Pick the flowers just as they open and use fresh.

In the Kitchen Use rosemary leaves in stocks, soups (especially potato), breads, marinades, butters or vinegars. Or try it with meat, stronger-flavored fish or vegetables, as well as egg and cheese dishes. With discretion, include rosemary leaves in fruit jams or jellies, fruit desserts, quick breads, cookies or sorbets.

Add the bare, dry stems to the coals when grilling. Add the flowers to salads or fruit desserts or use them to flavor sugar. Crystallize some leaves for decorating pastry.

Other Uses

Add the dried flowers or leaves to potpourris. Drink a tea made from the leaves to relieve indigestion. You can also use the tea as a gargle for sore throats, a rinse to make dark hair shiny, an addition to bathwater for stimulating circulation, a pain reliever for sore muscles or bruises, or an antiseptic cleaning solution.

In climates colder than Zone 8, dig up rosemary in the autumn and place in a container for indoor growing.

TIP Roasted potatoes are one of life's comfort foods. Simply cut potatoes into 1-inch pieces, toss with a little olive oil and minced rosemary, place on a baking sheet, and bake at 400°F for about 20 to 30 minutes or until tender, stirring occasionally.

SAFFRON

Crocus sativus
Iridaceae — iris family

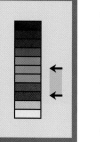

Saffron is the world's most expensive herb. Each flower produces only three of the red-orange stigmas, or the female part of the flower. Each one of the 14,000 of these stigmas needed to produce an ounce of dried saffron must be hand-picked.

Fortunately, only a pinch of saffron (the yield from six flowers) is added to most dishes. Don't add more saffron than called for in a recipe as too much causes a bitter taste. Saffron has a rich, spicy flavor that is traditional in Spanish paella, French bouillabaisse and Milanese risotto. It is also part of many European baked goods and northern Indian dishes, including desserts. Saffron has been a luxury item since the beginning of civilization, when it was used to dye royal robes. The word saffron is from the Arabic *za'fan*, for yellow; crocus is from the Greek *krokas*, for thread, alluding to the stigmas.

There is some contention over the best way to prepare saffron for recipes. For the richest flavor, cover a pinch of whole saffron with 2 teaspoons water for 5 minutes. Add ¼ cup lukewarm water and mix thoroughly but do not crush. Let stand for 2 hours before using. This method keeps the stigmas whole. A quicker method is to soak a pinch of whole saffron with 4 teaspoons water, then mash the threads, using the back of a metal spoon or mortar and pestle, until a thick paste is formed.

Description

Type Perennial corm. Zones 6 to 9.
Size 6 to 12 inches tall, 4 inches wide.
Flowers 6 lavender-purple petals to 2 inches long with an orange-red, three-branched stigma to 1¼ inches long. Autumn.
Leaves Stiff, grass-like, to 4 inches long, with white midrib.
Natural Habitat Probably southern Turkey.
Other Species and Cultivars Do not confuse saffron with the autumn-blooming meadow saffron, *Colchicum autumnale*, which is poisonous. Safflower or saffron thistle (*Carthamus tinctorius*) is sometimes used to adulterate powdered saffron. It is the dye source for the robes

Saffron crocus blooms in the autumn rather than the spring like most other crocuses. The bright red-orange stigmas are the part used for flavoring.

Unlike many herbs, it is saffron's stigmas (the part of the flower that catches pollen) that is used in cooking.

Of all the different kinds of crocus, only saffron is extensively used in cooking.

of Buddhist monks and nuns. The seeds supply safflower cooking oil.

How to Grow

Light Full sun to light shade.

Soil Well-drained.

Propagation After several years, dig up the clumps in late spring or early summer after the foliage has died down, separate the corms and replant immediately. Set corms 3 to 4 inches deep and 6 inches apart.

Care No special care is needed. The foliage appears in spring but dies back to the ground by summer. The leafless flowers appear in autumn.

In the Landscape Because of their diminutive size, plant saffron crocus where you'll be sure not to miss their beauty. A rock garden is ideal, but also consider planting them in patches at the base of shrubs or trees.

Culinary Uses

Harvest Snip the stigmas from the flowers when fully open. Preserve by drying. These must be stored in an airtight container in a cool, dark place. Use within a year.

In the Kitchen Use the stigmas with rice, cheese souffles, scrambled eggs, stews of fish, shellfish, poultry, lamb or beef. Or try with vegetables, tomato dishes, pastas, sweet breads, desserts with oranges, even ice cream. Combine with cardamom in sugar syrup, tea or coffee. Use to flavor vinegar, especially in conjunction with garlic and thyme.

Other Uses

Although saffron was once widely employed as a dye and medicine, these uses are seldom practiced today.

Considered the world's most expensive herb, saffron requires over 14,000 flowers to produce one dried ounce.

For rich saffron flavor, soak a pinch of saffron in water, keeping the stigmas whole.

Couscous with Vegetables and Saffron

2 tablespoons extra-virgin olive oil

1/2 cup diced onion

1 clove garlic, minced

2 cups vegetable stock or broth

1 cup fresh or frozen peas

A pinch of saffron, prepared in water

1/4 teaspoon hot red pepper sauce

1 cup couscous

1 cup peeled, seeded and diced tomatoes

In a saucepan, warm the oil over medium heat and stir in the onion and garlic. Cook, stirring, for about 5 minutes or until soft. Stir in the stock or broth, peas, saffron and pepper sauce. Cover and bring to a boil. Reduce heat and simmer for 10 minutes. Remove from heat and stir in couscous and tomato. Cover and let stand for 5 minutes. Serve immediately, garnishing with minced parsley or cilantro if desired. Makes six servings.

SAGE

Salvia officinalis
Labiatae — mint family

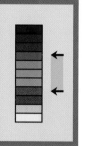

The textured, gray-green leaves of sage aren't just for Thanksgiving dressing. Try the fresh leaves with cornbread or tomato sauce.

Various cultivars of sage feature white, blue, violet or even pink flowers.

The pebbly, gray-green, suede-like leaves, spires of edible lavender flowers and citrusy, camphorous scent and flavor make sage a must-have in the culinary herb garden. Its uses go far beyond the Thanksgiving turkey stuffing so often prepared with dried sage. Experiment with fresh sage and its very different character. Intersperse leaves between the meat or vegetables on kebab skewers, drop a leaf into the water when cooking vegetables or dried beans, or mince some leaves into a fresh tomato sauce. Sage is a natural partner with cornmeal, be it in cornbread, pancakes or polenta. For an unusual hors d'oeuvre, batter and deep-fry the giant leaves of 'Berggarten' sage. In folklore and history, sage is the herb of immortality, health, wisdom and age.

Description

Type Woody, evergreen perennial. Zones 4 to 8.

Size 2 to 3 feet tall, 2 to 3 feet wide.

Flowers Whorls of $1/2$-inch lavender-blue flowers. Late spring to early summer.

Leaves Oval, pointed, gray-green, to 2 inches long.

Natural Habitat Native to northern Mediterranean coast.

Other Species and Cultivars Besides the common garden sage (*S. officinalis*), there are a number of other forms. 'Berggarten' and 'Holt's Mammoth' have extra-large leaves to 4 inches long and

Pineapple sage is delightful to use in the garden for both scent and flowers.

$1^1/_2$ inches wide on low, spreading plants. 'Compacta', 'Minimus' and 'Nana' have smaller leaves and shorter growth. There are also forms with colorful foliage that are beautiful additions to the garden, though somewhat less hardy and not as flavorful. These include: 'Purpurescens' with purplish leaves; 'Icterina' and 'Aurea' with yellow-and-green variegated leaves; and 'Tricolor' with the

Sage adapts well to containers, especially if fertilized monthly during the growing season.

leaves marked in white, pink and green.

Then there are the 900 or so other species of salvia, to say nothing of varieties. For culinary purposes, the most delightful ones are fruit sage (*S. dorisiana*) and pineapple sage (*S. elegans*). Both grow to 5 feet tall and are only hardy to Zone 9, but they can be grown as annuals elsewhere. Use the leaves in fruit salads, iced fruit drinks or desserts. Try the bright red flowers of pineapple sage in salads or as a garnish. 'Frieda Dixon' is a pineapple sage growing to 4 feet with salmon-pink flowers. The leaves of both also make wonderful additions to potpourris. Clary sage (*S. sclarea*) has leaves with a vanilla-balsam aroma. Make

TIP If you think that the Thanksgiving sage stuffing is overwhelming, try a light hand with the sage. Your stuffing will end up being fragrant and delicate...and more popular among your guests.

the leaves into fritters or add the flowers to salads.

The extra-large leaves of 'Berggarten' sage are great for making into sage-leaf fritters.

How to Grow
Light Full sun.
Soil Humus-rich, well-drained.
Propagation Sow seed indoors eight weeks before the last spring frost. Germination is erratic, but may be helped by freezing the seeds for three days prior to planting. Transplant outdoors one week before the last spring frost. Space 18 inches to 2 feet apart. Take cuttings, layer or divide in early summer after flowering.
Care Prune plants back after flowering to encourage fresh new growth. Control spider mites with horticultural soap and slugs with traps or barriers. Plants often become woody after five years or so and should be replaced.

In the Landscape Sage's foliage is a subtle foil to more colorful plants in the garden. When in bloom, it is as spectacular as any ornamental flower. The sages with colorful leaves bring that dimension to the garden and are especially fun to use in creating interesting color combinations.

The sages readily adapt to containers filled with a fast-draining potting mix and a monthly feeding with a balanced fertilizer according to the manufacturer's directions.

Try purple-leaved common sage in a planting with bronze fennel, purple fountain grass or other purple-foliage beauties.

Reminiscent of ornamental forms of sage, common sage also bears stems of striking blue flowers.

Bean and Vegetable Gratin

2 tablespoons extra-virgin olive oil
1 celery rib, thinly sliced
2 cloves garlic, minced
2 cups peeled, seeded and diced fresh tomatoes or a 14¹/₂-ounce can diced tomatoes
2 15-ounce cans white beans, rinsed and drained
2 cups diced summer squash
1 tablespoon minced fresh sage
¹/₂ cup fresh bread crumbs
¹/₂ cup grated Parmesan cheese
¹/₄ cup minced fresh parsley leaves
2 tablespoons extra-virgin olive oil
1 clove garlic, minced

Preheat oven to 350°F. In a large skillet, warm oil over medium heat and stir in celery. Cook, stirring about 5 minutes, or until soft. Stir in garlic and cook for 1 minute. Add tomatoes and cook, stirring occasionally, for 5 minutes. Remove from heat and stir in the beans, mashing about one fourth of them. Stir in squash and sage. Transfer to a 2-quart shallow baking dish. In a small bowl, combine crumbs, cheese, parsley, oil and garlic. Sprinkle over the bean mixture. Bake for 45 minutes or until the top is golden. Makes six servings.

Overwinter outdoors in a protected location and surrounded by mulch. Bring the dwarf forms indoors during the winter.

Culinary Uses

Harvest Gather the leaves at any time as needed. Preserve by drying. Pick the flowers as they open and use fresh.

In the Kitchen Include the leaves with vegetables, dried beans, cornbreads, pork, poultry, cheese, stuffings, butters, jellies or vinegars. Try the flowers in salads, fruit desserts or in hot apple cider.

Other Uses

Include fresh sprigs, particularly of the colorful types, in nosegays. Add the dried leaves to herb wreaths or crafts, especially in insect-repelling potpourris. Drink a tea made from the leaves to relieve indigestion, stress, coughs or colds, but do not take for more than two weeks at a time. Use the tea as a rinse for gray hair, as a facial tonic or as a deodorizing soak for feet.

Other forms of common sage include one with yellow-and-green variegated leaves and another with leaves of white, pink and green.

SALAD BURNET

Poterium sanguisorba (sometimes called *Sanguisorba minor*)
Rosaceae — rose family

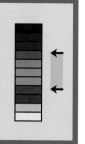

Salad burnet is one of the most underutilized of all culinary herbs. Its delicate cucumber flavor should become a staple in all your salads. As an added incentive, the leaves are a rich source of vitamin C. Plus, the flowers and seeds are edible. Four hundred years ago, people added a sprig of burnet to their glasses of red wine. Burnet blends particularly well with basil, dill, garlic chives, marjoram and thyme. The letters of Thomas Jefferson note that he had two boys pick six to eight bushels of burnet, not for a giant salad but for cattle pasture. In the garden salad burnet offers bright green mounds of delicate-looking, yet evergreen, foliage. Sir Francis Bacon recommended burnet for garden paths, along with mint and thyme, so that one could delight in all the fragrances.

Description
Type Perennial. Zones 4 to 8.
Size 1 to 2 feet tall, 1 to 2 feet wide.
Flowers Spherical heads of tiny pink flowers. Late spring.
Leaves Fern-like leaves with four to twelve pairs of rounded, toothed leaflets to 1 inch across.
Natural Habitat Native to western Asia and Europe.

Other Species and Cultivars
Great burnet (*Sanguisorba officinalis*, sometimes listed as *Poterium officinalis*) is a close relative used as an astringent medicinal herb.

How to Grow
Light Full sun to light shade.

Soil Humus-rich, well-drained.
Propagation Start seeds indoors six weeks before the last spring frost and plant outside one to two weeks before the last spring frost or sow directly into the garden no earlier than two weeks before the last spring frost. Space 1 foot apart. If allowed

Salad burnet, with its finely divided leaves, works well as an ornamental.

to go to seed, burnet self-sows. Divide the plants in spring.

Care Burnet needs very little attention. Remove flowers to keep the neat appearance. It grows best in the cool weather of spring and fall and may die in severe heat.

In the Landscape Salad burnet makes a naturally tidy edging plant in the garden. A bonus is that the plants are attractive almost year-round, and it brings fine texture to plantings.

You can grow salad burnet in a container filled with fast-draining potting mix and a monthly feeding with a balanced fertilizer according to the manufacturer's directions. Overwinter outdoors in a protected location with mulch around the pot.

Salad burnet grows well in containers. Overwinter it in a protected location outdoors, rather than inside.

Culinary Uses

Harvest Gather young, tender leaves as you need them. Do not use the older leaves as they tend to be bitter.

In the Kitchen Add minced leaves or seeds of salad burnet to coleslaw, potato salad, chicken salad, tuna salad, salad dressings, marinades for cooked vegetables, butters, cheese spreads, dips or vinegars. Include whole leaves in green salads, with sliced cucumbers or cooked beets with yogurt, in punches or wine coolers, or use them as garnish. Stuff poultry with the leaves and lemon slices. Use the flower in salads or as a garnish.

Other Uses

Dry the flowers for wreaths or other crafts. Make a tea from the leaves to relieve sunburn.

Spring Herb Cheese Spread

8 ounces cream cheese or homemade yogurt cheese
2 tablespoons minced fresh salad burnet
1 tablespoon minced fresh chives
1 tablespoon minced fresh chervil

Combine cheese, burnet, chives and chervil and blend well. Store in an airtight container in the refrigerator for at least eight hours to allow flavors to blend. Serve with crackers or vegetables for dipping. Makes 8 ounces.

Salad burnet's fern-like foliage, with its mild flavor of cucumbers, adds a wonderful touch to dips and cheese spreads.

SAVORY

Satureja species
Labiatae — mint family

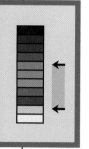

Summer savory (*S. hortensis*) and winter savory (*S. montana*) have a spicy flavor with elements of both thyme and oregano. The savories are a staple of French Mediterrean cooking and readily complement other flavorings of the region, especially garlic, bay and lemon. In Germany, savories are consider indispensible for cooking with both green and dried beans. Summer savory has the culinary edge over winter savory in that, with the exception of young leaves, it offers a milder taste. The advantage of winter savory is that you can harvest the leaves long after summer savory has died in the autumn.

The savories are among those enduring culinary herbs that have survived through the ages since ancient times. Their folklore includes stories of Greek satyrs wearing crowns of savory and that the savories were herbs of abundance, satiety and passion. In Medieval walled gardens, the savories were regularly interplanted with the vegetables.

Description

Type Summer savory is an annual. Winter savory is a woody, semi-evergreen perennial. Zones 5 to 10.

Winter savory forms compact, woody plants with stiff leaves that combine the flavors of thyme and oregano.

Size Winter savory grows to 1 foot tall and as wide. Summer savory grows to 18 inches tall and 1 foot wide.

Flowers Summer savory has 1/4-inch long, white to pink flowers in groups of three to six at the base of the upper leaves. Winter savory has 1/3-inch long, white to lavender flowers in spikes. Both bloom from midsummer until autumn.

Leaves Summer savory has narrow, dull green leaves to 1 inch long. Winter savory has narrow, glossy, dark, semi-evergreen leaves to 1 inch long.

Natural Habitat Both are native to the Mediterranean region.

Other Species and Cultivars Dwarf winter savory (*S. montana* 'Nana') grows to 4 to 8 inches tall and makes a diminutive edging in the garden. Creeping savory (*S. spicigera*) is similar to winter

savory, but with prostrate stems and a stronger flavor. Thyme-leaved savory (*S. thymbra*) has wiry, erect stems to 16 inches tall, pink flowers in early summer and a thyme-pennyroyal flavor.

How to Grow

Light Full sun.

Soil Well-drained soil. Summer savory needs soil that is more moist.

Propagation Start seeds of summer savory six weeks before the last frost and transplant outdoors after all danger of frost is past. Or, sow directly into the garden about a week before the last frost. Space 6 inches apart. Winter savory seeds are difficult to germinate, but you can try to start them indoors eight to ten weeks before the last spring frost. Transplant outdoors

Summer savory is an annual with soft green leaves. The flavor is milder than that of winter savory.

Fresh Tomato Sauce

2 cups peeled, seeded, and diced tomatoes
1 cup water
1/2 cup finely chopped sweet onion, such as vidalia
1 tablespoon minced fresh savory
4 tablespoons butter
1 tablespoon unbleached all-purpose flour
1/4 teaspoon salt
1/8 teaspoon ground black pepper

In a saucepan, combine tomatoes, water, onion and savory. Cook over medium-low heat 15 minutes or until the vegetables are soft. In a skillet, melt butter over medium heat, add flour and cook, stirring, for 1 minute. Slowly pour in tomato mixture, stirring constantly. Bring to a boil, reduce heat and simmer for 3 minutes or until thickened. Serve with pasta or as a sauce for grilled meat or vegetables. Makes four servings.

when all frost danger is past, spacing 10 inches apart. Take cuttings in early summer. Divide in spring or autumn. Layer in spring. Seeds of both savories germinate more quickly if soaked overnight in hot water before planting.

Care Summer savory needs good air circulation around it to prevent fungal diseases. To limit its sprawling tendencies, mound soil around the base of the stems. For winter savory, too much nitrogen in the soil or poor soil drainage in winter make it susceptible to diseases. Trim to shape in spring.

In the Landscape Summer savory tends to be a sprawling, nondescript herb. It makes an admirable foil for purple or tricolor sage, purple basil or nasturtiums. Winter savory's neat appearance and glossy leaves recommends it as an edging for beds or around focal points in the garden.

Both summer and winter savory adapt well to containers filled with fast-draining potting soil and a monthly feeding of a balanced fertilizer according to the manufacturer's directions. Both kinds may be brought indoors during the winter.

Culinary Uses

Harvest Pick sprigs of summer savory as needed. For drying, harvest before it flowers, cutting within several inches of the ground. Preserve by drying or freezing. Pick sprigs of winter savory as needed. For drying, cut stems back to 6 inches. Preserve by drying. Gather the flowers as they open.

In the Kitchen Use any of the leaves of summer savory or just the youngest leaves of winter savory with green or dried beans, peas, tomatoes, beets, winter root vegetables (such as turnips, rutabagas or parsnips), eggplant, any vegetables of the cabbage family, cheese, or any meat or fish. Add the leaves to soups, pâtés, hash, bouquet garni, salt-free herb blends, butters or vinegars. Use the flowers in salads or as a garnish.

Other Uses

Make a tea from the leaves of either winter or summer savory for stomach ailments. Use the tea in bathwater or facial tonics, or as a gargle for sore throats or a wash for insect bites.

Creeping savory is easy to grow in pots; bring them indoors in winter. Growing only 4 inches tall, this savory develops a mat of foliage.

SCENTED GERANIUM

Pelargonium species and cultivars
Geraniaceae — geranium family

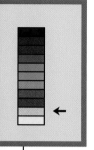

What's not to love about plants whose leaves have the scent of peppermint, chocolate mint, ginger, coconut, roses, lemon, lime, orange, nutmeg, apple, apricot, gooseberries, strawberries or peaches? Victorian ladies delighted in swishing their skirts against the foliage of scented geraniums, including a leaf in a letter, marking a favorite passage in a book or ringing a nosegay with the leaves. Modern gardeners derive no less pleasure. Scented geraniums are closely related to the brightly flowered annual geraniums, but have more subtly colored flowers, usually in shades of pink or white. In the kitchen, rose- and lemon-scented geraniums are the best for imparting their fragrance and flavor to desserts, jellies and drinks.

Among the lemon varieties, consider the old-fashioned lemon geraniums *P. crispum*, *P. crispum* 'Minor' and *P. crispum* 'Prince Rupert' plus its variegated form. Other lemon-scented ones are *P.* 'Frensham' and *P.* 'Mabel Grey'.

For a rose scent, consider the old-fashioned rose geranium, *P. graveolens*, also listed as *P.* x *asperum*, and its many forms including 'Grey Lady Plymouth', 'True Rose', 'Cinnamon Rose'

and 'Mint Rose'. Others are *P. capitatum* 'Attar of Roses' and *P.* 'Peacock'.

Can't make up your mind? Try *P.* 'Rober's Lemon Rose' or *P.* 'Dr. Livingstone' (also known as skeleton rose), which combine rose and lemon. Or try 'Lady Plymouth' with its rose, lemon and mint combination.

Description

Type Perennial. Zone 10.
Size 1 to 5 feet tall, 1 to 5 feet wide. Upright to sprawling.
Flowers Clusters of $^1/_2$- to $^3/_4$-inch flowers with five petals, white to bright pink, sometimes marked with a darker pink. Spring and early summer.
Leaves Velvety to crisp or slightly sticky. Triangular with scalloped to deeply indented edges, 1 to 4 inches across. Deep green, sometimes marked with a darker color or variegated.

Even the various sizes, shapes and colors of scented geranium leaves can't compare with the range of fragrances available.

Natural Habitat Native to South Africa.
Other Species and Cultivars About 200 species and cultivars of scented geraniums exist.

How to Grow

Light Full sun to light shade.

Scented geraniums make great container plants where their scent can be enjoyed by passers-by.

Rose Geranium Sorbet

12 rose geranium leaves
1¼ cups water
¾ cup granulated sugar
2 tablespoons lemon juice
1 large egg white

In a saucepan, combine leaves, water and sugar. Bring to a boil over medium-high heat, stirring to dissolve sugar. Remove from heat, cover and let steep for 30 minutes. Strain liquid into a bowl and add lemon juice. Pour into a shallow dish and freeze until mushy. Beat egg white until stiff. Remove the semi-frozen mixture from the freezer and fold in the egg white. Pour back into the dish and freeze for about an hour. Serve in dessert dishes and garnish with tiny geranium leaves or fresh geranium flowers. Makes four servings.

Note: For those who do not want to use the raw egg white, substitute powdered "Just Whites," available at grocery stores, according to the manufacturer's directions.

Culinary Uses

Harvest Pick leaves as needed. They are most fragrant just before blooming. Preserve by drying. Pick flowers as they open.

In the Kitchen Infuse applesauce, vanilla or rice pudding, sugar, honey, creme fraiche, sour cream or yogurt with the leaves. Make fruit sauces, jellies, sugar syrups, sorbets, vinegars or salad dressings. Place leaves on the bottom of cake pans before pouring in the batter. Add finely minced leaves to cookie, scones, cream cheese spreads or butters. Add leaves to a pot of black tea or use in punches. Add the fresh flowers to salads. Use them plain or crystallized to garnish desserts.

Other Uses

Include fresh leaves of any variety in nosegays or bouquets or the dried ones in potpourris or herb pillows. Make a tea from rose geranium leaves for menstrual problems or nausea. Add the tea to bathwater or use as a facial tonic.

Scented geraniums are mainly grown for their leaves, but they all do bear blooms—mostly in shades of pink.

Propagation Seed is very difficult to germinate. Propagate from cuttings in spring, summer or fall.

Care Water geraniums when the top ½ inch of soil is dry. Trim plants at any time to maintain size and shape, but an autumn pruning is especially helpful. Spray aphids or whiteflies with horticultural soap.

In the Landscape Place pots of scented geraniums near where you will often walk or sit. Group them all together for one massive combination of fragrances or, for a more moderate approach, group similar fragrances together in different locations around the garden. You can also train scented geraniums as standard topiaries.

In all but the warmest climates, grow scented geraniums in containers, keeping them outdoors in summer and bringing them indoors in winter. Nighttime winter temperatures must be below 60°F to flower. Use a fast-draining potting mix and a monthly feeding from spring to autumn of a balanced fertilizer according to the manufacturer's directions.

The old-fashioned rose geranium has been beloved since the late 1700's for its aromatic foliage.

SORREL

Rumex species
Polygonaceae — buckwheat family

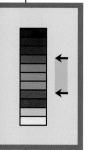

Garden (belleville) sorrel features large leaves that grow to 12 inches long.

Small, arrowhead-shaped leaves and low, mat-forming growth identify French (or buckler) sorrel.

Make an easy sauce for fish by sautéing minced sorrel and shallots in butter or olive oil.

Description

Type Perennial. Zones 4 to 8.

Size *R. acetosa* grows to 4 feet tall; *R. scutatus* grows 6 inches tall, forming a ground-hugging mat, then reaches 18 inches when in bloom. Both spread rapidly.

Flowers Slender, loose spikes of small, reddish flowers. Summer.

Leaves *R. acetosa* has oval, pointed leaves to 12 inches long and 2 inches wide. *R. scutatus* has arrowhead-shaped leaves to 4 inches long and 2 inches wide.

Natural Habitat Native to Europe, western Asia and northern Africa.

Other Species and Cultivars Roselle (*Hibiscus sabdariffa*) is commonly called sorrel in the Caribbean. It is a woody shrub with the red base of the flowers used in teas.

How to Grow

Light Full sun to light shade.

When obtaining sorrel from garden centers or speciality herb nurseries, note the botanical name instead of the common name. This is because there are two sorrels, both sometimes listed as French sorrel. The true French sorrel, also known as buckler sorrel, is *R. scutatus*. The other one, often called garden or belleville sorrel, is *R. acetosa*. Both have leaves with a tart, lemony flavor due to oxalic acid, but some people consider the true French version to be more refined. Both are high in vitamin A and contain other minerals and vitamins. Plus, they make rich food more digestible.

When preparing sorrel, it's important to cook it in a nonreactive pan such as stainless steel, enameled steel or nonstick. If cooked in iron or aluminum, sorrel turns an unappealing color and develops a bitter taste. Also, because of sorrel's high oxalic acid content, it should be eaten sparingly.

The classic way to use sorrel is in a soup made with potatoes and served either hot or cold.

Sow sorrel seed in spring, directly into the garden. Easy!

Soil Humus-rich, moist, well-drained.

Propagation Sow seed in spring directly into the garden several weeks before the last spring frost. Germination takes about a week. Space plants 1 foot apart. Divide in autumn at least every three years to help maintain vigorous plantings.

Care Protect sorrel from slugs with traps or barriers.

In the Landscape The larger leaves of garden sorrel make a bolder statement in the garden. Both types quickly spread. Choose a site carefully so that their invasive tendencies are not a problem.

Growing sorrel in containers is a good way to limit its spreading ways. Use a fast-draining potting mix and a monthly feeding during the growing season with a balanced fertilizer according to the manufacturer's directions. Overwinter in a protected place with a mulch around the pot.

Sorrel Soup

3 leeks (about ¾ pound), white part washed, drained and thinly sliced
2 tablespoons canola oil
1 sweet potato (about ½ pound), peeled and cut into ½-inch pieces
2 cups vegetable stock or broth
1 cup water
¼ pound fresh sorrel, washed, stems discarded and leaves cut crosswise into thin strips
⅓ cup low-fat or non-fat sour cream
1 tablespoon lemon juice

In a large saucepan, warm the oil over medium-low heat. Stir in the leeks. Cook, stirring occasionally, about 5 minutes or until softened. Add potato, stock or broth, and water. Cover and simmer for about 15 minutes or until potato pieces are tender. In a blender, purée the potato mixture with the sorrel in two batches until very smooth. Be sure to hold lid tightly. Transfer to a bowl and whisk in the sour cream. Add additional water if necessary for desired consistency. Chill soup in an air-tight container for at least two hours. Just before serving stir in the lemon juice. Garnish with thin strips of sorrel. Makes four servings.

Culinary Uses

Harvest Gather leaves as needed. The youngest leaves on garden sorrel taste the best in late spring to midsummer. Remove the midrib before using. Sorrel does not preserve well.

In the Kitchen Add leaves to tossed green or potato salads. Add minced leaves to vegetable soup, omelettes, quiches, lamb, fish or smoked fish spreads. Try in sauces for fish, poultry or pork.

Other Uses

Crush the leaves and use to bleach rust, mold or ink stains from linen, wicker or silver. Make a poultice of the leaves for boils or wounds.

Sorrel is prized for the tart, lemony flavor in the leaves. Those leaves are high in vitamins and minerals, and aid digestion.

SWEET CICELY

Myrrhis odorata
Umbelliferae — carrot family

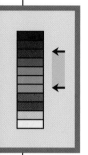

Sweet cicely's soft-textured leaves are one of the harbingers of spring. With a sweet flavor that combines anise and celery, sweet cicely complements most root vegetables and cabbage family members. It's also quite useful in baking because the sweet taste reduces the amount of sugar needed. This is especially advantageous with tart fruits like rhubarb or gooseberries. Reduce the amount of sugar by about half when you add a tablespoon of sweet cicely leaves. After the white flowers finish blooming in late spring, clusters of 1-inch seeds develop. These, either green or ripened to a shiny brown, bring their own spicy flavor to desserts. After plants grow at least a year, you can dig up the roots and eat them as a raw or cooked vegetable. But who can bear to remove any of these graceful plants that bring such beauty to the shaded garden?

Description

Type Perennial. Zones 3 to 7.
Size 3 feet tall, 2 feet wide.
Flowers Flat clusters, 2 to 3 inches across, of tiny white flowers. Late spring.
Leaves Fern-like, with finely divided leaflets, whitish on the underside.

Natural Habitat Native to Europe.

How to Grow

Light Light shade.
Soil Humus-rich, moist, well-drained.

Propagation Seed is difficult to germinate, but you may find success by planting fresh seed outdoors in late summer or early fall. Divide in spring or autumn, making sure each piece of root has a growth bud. Space plants 2 feet apart.

As its name implies, sweet cicely's sweet taste reduces the amount of sugar you'll need to use in many recipes.

Looking almost like a fern, sweet cicely brings soft, delicate texture to the landscape.

Care Sweet cicely requires cool, moist, shady conditions; it will not tolerate sun. Allow some of the seeds to remain on the plant, as they often self-sow.

In the Landscape With the filigree foliage and white flowers, sweet cicely is a welcome addition to shaded flower borders as well as the herb garden.

Culinary Uses

Harvest Pick sweet cicely leaves as needed. Preserve by freezing. Harvest the seeds when they ripen to a shiny, dark brown. Preserve seeds by drying.

In the Kitchen Add the leaves to salads, cream or fruit soups, stews, bouquet garni, vegetables, eggs, butters, vinegars, wine drinks, cakes, cookies or fruit desserts. Stuff a whole fish with the leaves before baking, grilling or poaching. Include the chopped green seeds in fruit salads, fruit pies, sugar syrups or ice cream. Add the crushed ripe seed in fruit dishes, sugar syrups, cakes or liqueurs.

Use the ridged seeds of sweet cicely fresh or dried. Like the foliage, they have a delicate, anise-like flavor.

Other Uses

Use the fresh leaves in bouquets or the dried leaves in potpourris. Include the dried seed heads in wreaths or crafts. Mix the ground seeds with beeswax for a wood furniture polish. Drink a tea made from the leaves for indigestion or coughs.

In late spring, sweet cicely shows off a crown of creamy white flower clusters.

Apple Salad

2 ripe apples, such as 'Gayla'
2 tablespoons lemon juice
1/2 cup thinly sliced lovage stems and/or minced fresh leaves
1/4 cup minced fresh sweet cicely leaves
1/2 cup toasted coarsely chopped pecans
1/2 cup mayonnaise
Bibb lettuce leaves

Core and quarter the apples, then dice. Put in a bowl and toss with the lemon juice to coat. Stir in the lovage, sweet cicely and pecans. Cover and chill in the refrigerator for at least 1 hour. Stir the mayonnaise into the apple mixture, combining well. Serve on a bed of lettuce. Makes four servings.

SWEET MARJORAM

Origanum majorana
Labiatae — mint family

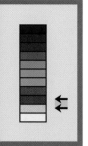

Marjoram does well in containers.

Description

Type Perennial. Zones 9 to 10. May be grown as an annual.

Size 1 foot tall, 6 inches wide.

Flowers The knotted flower buds open to tiny white or pink blooms. Late summer to early autumn.

Leaves Oval, pale gray-green, velvety leaves $1/4$ to 1 inch long.

Natural Habitat Native to northern Africa and southwest Asia.

How to Grow

Light Full sun.

Soil Well-drained.

Propagation Start seeds indoors eight weeks before the last spring frost. Transplant outdoors after all danger of frost is passed. Space 6 to 8 inches apart. Divide in spring or autumn. Take cuttings in summer.

Care Pinch the growing tips out to encourage branching.

In the Landscape Sweet marjoram is a good companion to some of the other Mediterranean herbs such as winter savory, sage, thyme and oregano.

Grow sweet marjoram in a container filled with fast-draining potting mix and a monthly feeding with a

Kept trimmed back, sweet marjoram will form a compact ground cover.

Sweet marjoram is a gray-green herb with the flower buds looking like silvery "knots" at the tips of its stems. This gives rise to another common name, knotted marjoram. Sweet marjoram has a sweet-and-savory fla-

vor that is a mild-mannered version of its cousin oregano. There is much botanical confusion in this family, so that what you buy as sweet marjoram may actually be hardy marjoram (*O.* x *majoricum*), otherwise known as Italian oregano. The taste is similar but is more closely allied to the pungent oreganos. The only sure way to identify sweet marjoram is by the knotted buds. To best appreciate sweet marjoram's delicate flavor, use it in simple dishes where it is not over-ruled. Add it toward the end of cooking so that the essential oils do not evaporate.

For some reason, the ancient Roman poet and philosopher Lucretius was not particularly fond of marjoram, writing "amaricinum fugitat sus." Translated: swine shun marjoram.

Golden marjoram, which is actually more of an ornamental oregano, brightens the garden with its foliage.

Sweet marjoram's stem tips look like knots.

mushrooms and tomatoes. Sweet marjoram is also good with cheese or egg dishes, fish, poultry or pork.

Culinary Uses

Harvest Gather sprigs of leaves as needed. To harvest for drying, cut plants back to 2 inches tall just before

balanced fertilizer according to the manufacturer's directions. Bring plants indoors in the autumn.

blooming. In warm climates, gardeners may get several cuttings but those in colder areas usually get only one.

In the Kitchen Add the fresh leaves to salads or incorporate them into butters, vinegars, marinades or salad dressings. Among the vegetables that complement sweet marjoram are fennel, celeriac, carrots, lima beans, eggplant,

Other Uses

For a wonderfully scented furniture polish, rub wood furniture with the fresh leaves. Include the flowers in nosegays. Add the dried leaves to potpourris or use the dried flowers in crafts. Make a tea from the leaves for indigestion, insomnia, stress, colds, coughs or headaches. Add the tea to bathwater or use as a hair rinse or mouthwash. Make a compress for painful muscles or joints.

Vegetable Stew

2 tablespoons canola oil
1 cup diced onion
1 cup thinly sliced celery
2 cloves garlic, minced
2 cups sliced mushrooms
1 1/2 cups thinly sliced carrots
1/2 pound small new potatoes, quartered
2 cups peeled, seeded and diced tomatoes
1 cup vegetable stock or broth
1/2 teaspoon salt
1/4 teaspoon freshly ground black pepper
2 teaspoons minced fresh sweet marjoram

In a large skillet, warm oil over medium heat. Stir in onion, celery and garlic. Cook, stirring occasionally, about 5 minutes or until the vegetables are softened. Stir in the mushrooms and cook for another 5 minutes. Stir in the carrots, potatoes, tomatoes, stock or broth, salt and pepper. Cover and reduce heat to low, then simmer for 30 minutes or until the potatoes and carrots are tender. Remove the cover, add the marjoram. Simmer for another 10 minutes. Makes six servings.

Recognize sweet marjoram by its gray-green, velvety leaves and knotted flower buds.

TARRAGON

Artemisia dracunculus var. sativa
Compositae — daisy family

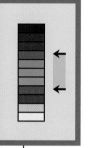

You could describe tarragon's flavor as that of a spicy anise. Long favored in French cooking, tarragon also makes an excellent addition to herb blends.

In the culinary realm, tarragon is generally understood to be French tarragon (the one with the snappy anise flavor), not the Russian tarragon (*A. dracunulus* subsp. *dracunculoides*) which has very little flavor. Because French tarragon is sterile, meaning it cannot produce seeds, you can only propagate it from cuttings or division. Tarragon seeds yield only Russian tarragon. Tarragon is one of the fresh herbs in the classic French quartet, *fines herbes*, along with chervil, parsley and chives. Tie these together in a little bouquet to flavor a cooked dish or mince together and add to butter, an omelet or a sauce. Use tarragon with a light hand and add it near the end of cooking to prevent it from becoming bitter. The exception here: recipes baked in liquid or when tarragon is tucked beneath the skin of poultry before roasting.

Description
Type Perennial. Zones 4 to 8.
Size 2 feet tall, 2 feet wide.
Flowers Tiny, globe-shaped, yellow to greenish-white flowers. Summer.
Leaves Narrow, lance-shaped, dull green leaves 1 to 4 inches long and $1/4$ inch wide.
Natural Habitat Native to the area around the Caspian Sea and Siberia.
Other Species and Cultivars Gardeners in hot, humid climates who have not been successful growing tarragon often substitute Mexican tarragon (*Tagetes lucida*). To learn more about that herb, see page 108.

How to Grow
Light Full sun to light shade.

Tarragon has two odd traits. One—if you chew a leaf, your tongue will go numb.
Two—the roots tend to grow in a serpentine or "dragon-like" fashion, which gave rise to the species name. These entangled roots constrict the plant, which is why tarragon needs division so often.

With stems clothed in narrow leaves, tarragon adds another textural element to the herb garden.

Tarragon Cheese Spread

1 tablespoon butter
1 tablespoon unbleached all-purpose flour
1/2 cup milk
4 ounces grated Monterey Jack cheese
1 tablespoon capers, drained *(optional)*
1 tablespoon minced fresh tarragon leaves

In a small skillet, melt the butter over medium heat. Stir in the flour and cook, stirring, for 1 minute. Gradually add the milk, stirring constantly. Cook about 2 minutes or until thickened. Remove from the stove and stir in the cheese, capers and tarragon. Put into an air-tight container and chill. Serve on crackers. Makes 1 cup.

Soil Humus-rich, well-drained.

Propagation French tarragon cannot be started from seed. Divide in early spring. Take cuttings in midsummer. Space plants 2 feet apart.

Care Pinch out the growing tips several times during the growing season to increase branching. French tarragon needs well-drained soil, especially in winter. To maintain vigor, divide plants every two or three years. Provide a winter mulch or grow tarragon as an annual.

In the Landscape French tarragon tends to flop and sprawl, so it is not the most ornamental of herbs. Still, the plant has a fine texture that serves as a foil to bolder plants and it is one of the first herbs up in the spring. It is also said to enhance the growth of vegetables.

French tarragon grows well in a container filled with a fast-draining potting mix and a monthly feeding with a balanced fertilizer according to the manufacturer's directions. If brought indoors during the winter, it needs very bright light. To overwinter outdoors, put in a protected spot and surround the plant and pot with mulch.

Culinary Uses

Harvest Gather leaves as needed. Preserve by freezing. Although flavor is diminished with drying, the dried leaves are useful in salt-free herb blends because of their high mineral content.

In the Kitchen Tarragon is especially complementary to fish, shellfish and chicken. It is also traditional in béarnaise, hollandaise, rémoulade and tartar sauces. Be sure to try the leaves in salad dressings, soups, rice or grains, eggs, vegetables, salt-free herb blends, butters, vinegars or liqueurs.

Other Uses

Drink a tea made from the leaves as a healthful tonic, to aid digestion or to stimulate appetite.

The name tarragon is taken from the French esdragon, *or little dragon, referring to the tangled, serpent-like roots that develop as plants age.*

Add tarragon leaves to vinegar to make your own personalized "house" version!

THYME

Thymus species and cultivars
Labiatae — mint family

In culinary terms, thyme might be called a universal herb, as it goes with just about everything and rounds out the flavor of other herbs that accompany it. The same might be said of its role in the garden, as the low-growing, spreading thymes serve to pull together the disparate elements in the garden. And there is no small number of thymes from which to choose, what with some 350 species and dozens upon dozens of varieties. There is much confusion over correct botanical identification as well as different plants having the same common name. And many thymes have no culinary value, although they may be stunning in the garden or have medicinal qualities. Thymes have long been associated with fairies, so perhaps they are responsible for such confusion. Fortunately, thyme is also considered to give strength and courage, so a cup of thyme tea will fortify you as you consider the choices.

Description

Type Evergreen to semi-evergreen woody perennial.

Hardiness varies, depending on the species and cultivar.

Size Common thyme and lemon thyme grow to 12 inches tall. Broad-leaved thyme grows to 8 inches tall. Creeping thyme, caraway thyme and mother-of-thyme grow 2 to 3 inches tall.

Flowers Small clusters of $1/4$-inch lavender, rose, pink or white flowers. Summer.

Leaves Oval to lance-shaped, pointed, $1/4$ to $1/2$ inch long. Smooth, dark green to velvety gray, also variegated.

Natural Habitat Native to the western Mediterrean.

Thyme is pleasant to behold, and the perfect herb for so many culinary dishes.

Creeping (wild) thyme forms a dense mat on the ground and bears flowers in shades of mauve to magenta.

Other Species and Cultivars

The most widely used culinary thyme is common thyme (*T. vulgaris*), hardy in Zones 7 to 8, with tiny, stiff, gray-green leaves on some-

Creeping thyme makes a beautiful and edible groundcover.

what upright stems and white to pinkish-lavender flowers. The form called English, German or winter thyme has a somewhat stronger flavor and is more hardy than the more sweetly flavored form called French or summer thyme. There are also variegated forms.

Broad-leaved thyme (*T. pulegioides*), also sometimes listed as mother-of-thyme, is hardy in Zones 4 to 8. It is intensely aromatic with soft, broad, green leaves on sprawling stems and pink to purple flowers.

Creeping thyme (*T. praecox*), also listed as wild thyme, has a typical thyme scent and flavor. Hardy in Zones 5 to 8, it forms a thick mat on the ground with tiny leaves and mauve to magenta flowers. Mother-of-thyme (*T. serpyllum*), also listed as wild thyme and creeping thyme, is very similar but hardy in

Zones 4 to 8. Tiny leaves cover the prostrate stems. The many forms of this species are often grown more as ornamentals because of their colorful flowers, although you can use leaves in cooking.

Caraway thyme (*T. herba-barona*), hardy in Zones 6 to 8, is another low-spreading species. But the tiny green leaves have a scent and flavor of caraway. The flowers are bright mauve. There are also forms with the character of nutmeg or lemon.

As good as the traditional thyme flavor may be, more and more people are turning to the various lemon-flavored thymes. These versions add a piquant twist to this herb that enhances food even more. Lemon thyme (*T. x citriodorus*), hardy in Zones 7 to 9, is a variable hybrid between *T. vulgaris* and *T. pulegioides*. There are a number of variegated forms with

Eggplant and Zucchini with Thyme

3 tablespoons extra-virgin olive oil
1 medium onion, thinly sliced
1 pound eggplant, cut into 1-inch cubes
1 pound zucchini, thinly sliced
1 pound tomatoes, peeled, seeded and diced
1 tablespoon minced fresh thyme leaves
2 cloves garlic, minced
1/2 teaspoon salt
1/4 teaspoon freshly ground black pepper

In a large skillet, preferably non-stick, warm the oil over medium heat. Stir in the onion and cook, stirring occasionally, for 5 minutes or until softened. Stir in the eggplant and zucchini. Reduce heat to low and cook, stirring occasionally, for 10 minutes. Stir in the tomatoes, thyme, garlic, salt and pepper. Cover and cook for 20 minutes or until the vegetables are tender. Serve immediately. Makes six servings.

Common thyme's cascading stems soften the edges of container plantings.

gold, yellow or white accents. In addition, there are lemon forms of creeping thyme and caraway thyme.

Among the other "flavored" thymes are coconut, lavender, oregano and nutmeg. The ones with the greatest culinary potential are 'Orange Balsam' and 'Orange Spice', both with a strong character of oranges.

Of the many other thymes grown as ornamentals, one of the more delightful is woolly thyme (*T. pseudolanuginosus*), hardy in Zones 6 to 8. Growing only 1 to 3 inches tall, it forms thick mats of velvety gray leaves.

How to Grow
Light Full sun to light shade.
Soil Well-drained.

Propagation Start seed of species indoors six to eight weeks before the last frost in spring. Germination is best at 70°F and takes about a week. Space plants 1 foot apart. Divide or take cuttings in spring.

Care Trim plants in early spring to remove any dead growth and to encourage new branches. Trim again after flowering. Common thyme may become so woody after several years that it is best to replace it. Spray spider mites with horticultural soap.

In the Landscape Place the more upright-growing forms of common thyme near the edges of herb beds where it can be readily reached, since it is used so often in cooking. Allow the taller, trailing types to spread across the ground, but don't forget to use them along the edges of raised beds or trailing over low walls. Plant the very short creeping types between stepping stones.

Thymes fill a container and cascade over the edges beautifully. Use a fast-draining potting mix and feed

Although there are a number of varieties of thyme, almost all of them are perfect for planting near the edges of beds or low walls.

Common thyme is a low-growing, shrubby plant with small, flavorful leaves and white to pale purple flowers in summer.

as most vegetables. Try the leaves with cheese or fish dishes, rice and grains, beans or breads. Caraway thyme makes a great partner with sauerkraut, beef and pork. And, surprisingly, the lemon- or orange-flavored thymes are also intriguing additions to desserts and sweets, especially fruit compotes, fruit pies and jellies. The fresh flowers are a colorful, subtly flavored garnish or addition to salads.

Other Uses

Include the fresh stems or flowers in nosegays. Add the dried leaves or flowers in potpourri or insect-repelling mixtures. Drink a tea made from the leaves to relieve indigestion, insomnia, coughs, hay fever, colds or sore throat. Or use as a facial tonic, hair rinse for dandruff, mouthwash, wash for insect bites or wounds, or addition to the bathwater for sore muscles or aching joints. Do not use internally as a medicine when pregnant.

monthly with a balanced fertilizer according to the manufacturer's directions.

stuffings. Thyme enhances poultry, fish, shellfish, beef, pork or lamb as well

Culinary Uses

Harvest Gather stems as needed, stripping off the leaves for cooking. Harvest for drying is best done just before flowering. To preserve, dry or freeze.

In the Kitchen With what can thyme not be used? Add the leaves to salads, stock, sauces, soups, stews, butters, vinegars, marinades, salad dressings or

Golden lemon thyme is one of several thyme varieties featuring leaves with a citrusy flavor and fragrance.

Cranberry Sauce with Thyme

1/2 cup sugar
1/4 cup orange juice
1/4 cup orange-flavored liqueur
8 ounces fresh cranberries
1 tablespoon minced orange zest
1 tablespoon minced thyme

In a saucepan, combine the sugar, orange, juice and liqueur. Place over low heat and cook, stirring frequently, until the sugar is dissolved. Add the cranberries and increase the heat to medium. Bring to a boil and simmer for 5 minutes, stirring occasionally, or until the berries begin to burst. Remove from the heat and stir in the orange zest and the thyme. Cool, then store in an air-tight container in the refrigerator. Makes 2 1/2 cups.

VIOLA, VIOLET

Viola species and cultivars
Violaceae — violet family

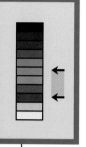

For a flower so diminutive, violets capture the heart like few others. For thousands of years, they have played a role in folklore, perfume and romance, to say nothing of kitchens. Nothing is so cheery a garnish as a sprinkling of violets. And these flowers are usually the first, if not the only, flower that people think of crystallizing. What is not as widely known is that you can steep sweet violets (*V. odorata*) with their sweetly perfumed flavor, and use the liquid to make jelly, dessert syrup or sorbet.

The Johnny-jump-up (*V. tricolor*), often with a bi-colored "face", offers no scent, but you can use the wintergreen-flavored flowers as a fresh or crystallized garnish.

Description

Type *V. odorata* is an evergreen perennial in Zones 6 to 9. *V. tricolor*

Intensely fragrant, double-flowered Parma violets are the treasures of the sweet violet world. Consider the lavender-blue 'Duchesse de Parme', lavender 'Lady Hume Campbell', white 'Swanley White' or deep lavender 'Marie Louise' for your garden.

Although an annual, Johnny-jump-ups readily self-sow, meaning that you'll always have new plants coming along.

is a perennial that readily self-sows.

Size *V. odorata* grows to 6 inches tall and 12 inches wide. *V. tricolor* grows to 1 foot tall and 8 inches wide.

Flowers Half-inch flowers with five unequal petals of the same or different colors. *V. odorata* is available in shades of purple, rose and white. They are usually all of one color, but may be shaded. *V. tricolor* most often has, as the species name implies, blooms with the three colors of purple, yellow and white; some cultivars have just one shade or some variation. Both types bloom mainly in spring, with some repeat in autumn.

Leaves *V. odorata* has oval to heart-shaped leaves, to 2¹/₂ inches wide, arising from a rosette of leaves that spread by runnes called stolons. *V. tricolor* has oval to lance-shaped leaves with toothed or lobed edges.

Natural Habitat Native to Europe, Asia and North Africa.

Other Species and Cultivars

The most widely available cultivars of *V. odorata* are the dark purple 'Royal Robe', pink 'Rosina' and 'White Czar'. Over 500 other species of viola are native throughout the temperate regions of the world and hundreds more varieties exist as well.

Pansies are a large-flowered version of sweet violets and Johnny-jump-ups. Pansies are a staple of the spring and autumn garden.

Crystallized viola petals are both beautiful and delicious.

Violet Syrup

1 cup sweet violets
2 cups water
Granulated sugar

Cut or pinch off the calyx of each violet (the green part directly behind the petals). In a saucepan, combine the flowers and the water. Bring to a boil over medium-high heat. Reduce heat and simmer gently for 30 minutes. Pour into a bowl, cover and let steep overnight. Strain and measure the remaining liquid. Put the liquid in a saucepan with an equal quantity of sugar. Cook over medium heat and bring to a boil. Boil, stirring, for 10 minutes. Let cool and store in an air-tight container in the refrigerator. Serve over fresh fruit or ice cream or fold into whipped topping. Makes about 1 cup.

How to Grow

Light Full sun to light shade.

Soil Humus-rich, moist, well-drained.

Propagation To start sweet violets from seed, place the seed in an airtight bag in the freezer for several days. Then sow the seed indoors eight to ten weeks before the last spring frost. Transplant seedlings or directly sow seeds outdoors about a week before the last spring frost. Seeds germinate in one to three weeks. Divide in spring or autumn.

To start Johnny-jump-ups, sow seed outdoors in fall in areas that get no frost for bloom during the winter; in colder areas, sow seed outdoors in autumn or spring. Or start seed indoors in early winter in any area for transplanting outdoors in spring. Plants readily self-sow once established.

Care Temperature regulates violet blooms; they need cool nights, such as in spring or autumn, to initiate flowering. Plants will bloom somewhat longer if you remove the faded flowers. Control spider mites with horticultural soap.

In the Landscape Violets look charming planted beneath shrubs, with spring-blooming bulbs or near a walkway where they can be appreciated every day.

Both sweet violets and Johnny-jump-ups readily grow in containers filled with a fast-draining potting mix and a monthly feeding with a balanced fertilizer according to the manufacturer's directions. Plants and seedlings readily overwinter outdoors in containers to Zone 6.

Culinary Uses

Harvest The leaves are most tender and have the best flavor in spring. Pick the flowers as they open. The flowers are best used fresh or preserved by crystallizing.

In the Kitchen Toss the leaves of sweet violet into salads or make a tea from the leaves for the liquid in desserts. Remove the green part directly behind sweet violet petals and crystallize the flowers or sprinkle whole or minced over food as a fresh garnish. Also use them in flavoring vinegar, sugar or butter. Or make a tea from them for use in drinks, syrups, honey, jellies or sorbet.

The petals of Johnny-jump-ups have very little flavor; but with the green sepal behind the petals, the flowers have a wintergreen flavor. Use them fresh as a garnish in fruit salads or drinks, or crystallized for decorating pastries.

Other Uses

No flower is better suited to nosegays or bouquets. Use the pressed flowers in craft projects. Include the dried flowers in potpourris. Make a tea from the leaves or flowers of the sweet violet or Johnny-jump-up for coughs or colds or to remove toxins. Add the tea to bathwater or use as a facial tonic or hair rinse.

The little "faces" of Johnny-jump-ups endear them to gardeners. Plus they make bright additions to salads and serve as beautiful garnishes for desserts.

SOURCES

Akin Back Farm
2501 Highway 53 South
LaGrange, KY 40031
Extensive plant list
Catalog $3

Companion Plants
7247 North Coolville Ridge
   Road
Athens, OH 45701
Extensive plant and seed list
Catalog $3

Dabney Herbs
PO Box 22061
Louisville, KY 40252
Extensive plant list
Catalog $2

Edgewood Farm Nursery
RR 2, Box 303
Stanardsville, VA 22973
Unusual herbs and perennials
Catalog $2

Edible Landscaping
PO Box 77
Afton, VA 22920
Source of kaffir lime plus other
   herbs and unusual food plants
Catalog free

**The Flowery Branch Seed
Company**
PO Box 1330
Flowery Branch, GA 30542
Extensive seed list
Catalog $4

**Fox Hollow Seed
Company**
PO Box 148
McGrann, PA 16236-0148
Extensive seed list
Catalog $1

Goodscents Gardens
652 Panda Road
Washougal, WA 98671
Extensive plant list
Catalog $1

Goodwin Creek Garden
PO Box 83
Williams, OR 97544
Extensive plant and seed list
Catalog $1

Greenfield Herb Garden
PO Box 9
Shipshewana, IN 46565
Herb seeds and plants
Catalog $1.50 and SASE

Herbs-Liscious
1702 South Sixth Street
Marshalltown, IA 50158
Extensive plant list
Catalog $2

Johnny's Selected Seeds
1 Foss Hill Road
RR 1, Box 2580
Albion, ME 04910-9731
Extensive seed list
Catalog free

Logee's Greenhouses
141 North Street
Danielson, CT 06239-1939
Unusual herbs plus tropical
   plants, including curry leaf
   and Parma violets
Catalog $3

NaAuSay Farm
71 Timberlake Trail
PO Box 304
Oswego, IL 60543
Extensive plant list
Catalog $3

Nichols Garden Nursery
1190 North Pacific Highway N. E.
Albany, OR 97321-4580
Plants and seeds
Catalog free

Northwoods Nursery
27635 South Oglesby Road
Canby, OR 97013
Unusual herbs
Catalog $3

**Peaceful Valley Farm
Supply**
PO Box 2209
Grass Valley, CA 95945
Organic gardening supplies
Catalog free

Pinetree Garden Seeds
Box 300
New Gloucester, ME 04260
Seeds in small packets
Catalog free

**Renaissance Acres
Organic Herb Farm**
4450 Valentine Road
Whitmore Lake, MI 48189-9691
Extensive plant list
Catalog $3

Richter's Herbs
357 Highway 47
Goodwood, Ontario
Canada L0C 1A0
Incredible plant and seed list
Catalog $2.50

**Sandy Mush Herb
Nursery**
316 Surrett Cove Road
Leicester, NC 28748-5517
Extensive plant and seed list
Catalog $4

Seeds of Change
PO Box 15700
Santa Fe, NM 87506-5700
Organic seeds
Catalog free

Shepherd's Garden Seeds
30 Irene Street
Torrington, CT 06790-6658
Seeds and plants
Catalog free

**Southern Exposure Seed
Exchange**
PO Box 170
Earlysville, VA 22936
Extensive seed list
Catalog $2

Sunnyboy Gardens
3314 Earlysville Road
Earlysville, VA 22936
Extensive plant list
Catalog $3

The Thyme Garden
20546 Alsea Highway
Alsea, OR 97324
Extensive plant and seed list
Catalog $2

Well-Sweep Herb Farm
317 Mt. Bethel Road
Port Murray, NJ 07865
Extensive plant list
Catalog $2

**Wrenwood of Berkeley
Springs**
Route 4, Box 361
Berkeley Springs, WV 25411
Extensive plant list
Catalog $2.50

INDEX